How to Weed Your Attic

How to Weed Your Attic

Getting Rid of the
Junk without Destroying History

Elizabeth H. Dow
Lucinda P. Cockrell

ROWMAN & LITTLEFIELD
Lanham • Boulder • New York • London

Published by Rowman & Littlefield
A wholly owned subsidary of The Rowman & Littlefield Publishing Group, Inc.
4501 Forbes Boulevard, Suite 200, Lanham, Maryland 20706
www.rowman.com

Unit A, Whitacre Mews, 26-34 Stannary Street, London SE11 4AB

British Library Cataloguing in Publication Information Available

Library of Congress Cataloging-in-Publication Data Available

Library of Congress Control Number: 2018947882

ISBN 978-1-5381-1546-6 (cloth: alk. paper)
ISBN 978-1-5381-1547-3 (electronic)

∞™ The paper used in this publication meets the minimum requirements of
American National Standard for Information Sciences—Permanence of Paper
for Printed Library Materials, ANSI/NISO Z39.48-1992.

Printed in the United States of America

To Polly Darnell

Contents

Acknowledgments

Elizabeth: In the late 1980s, I worked with Polly Darnell at the Henry Sheldon Museum of Vermont History in Middlebury, Vermont. During our two years together, she helped me develop a public presentation that focused on how to distinguish family papers that have historical value from those that don't. I have delivered it, from time to time, ever since. Without that background, this book would never have materialized. I'm very grateful to Polly's help in that fledgling effort—and many other endeavors.

I wrote a draft of the book before I retired from Louisiana State University, but events conspired to make finishing it impossible. A couple years into retirement in Vermont, however, the unfinished manuscript drew me back. Realizing I needed a museum professional to complement my archival knowledge, I turned to a colleague from my time at LSU, who had also retired to Vermont. I asked if she would join the effort. I'm very grateful for her willingness to share her invaluable collaboration.

Lucinda: Thanks to my husband, Dale, for advice, direction, and support in all things. Thanks to my parents who gave me my love of history, a collecting disposition, and many opportunities of attic weeding—learning how to winnow the historically significant wheat from the chaff.

Polly Darnell and Dr. Neil Stout applied their editor eyes to the entire text, and their comments made it much better.

Finally, our editor, Charles Harmon, provided steadfast and prompt help every time we called on him; we're very grateful.

Heartfelt thanks to you all. Regardless of all the outside help and advice, we made the final decisions about the book, and any weaknesses or inadequacies it exhibits come from us.

Preface

In Riel Nason's book *All the Things We Leave Behind*, a young man on the brink of taking over his family's roadside antiques business muses, "It's true that you can't take it with you, and something has to be done with all the things we leave behind. Families keep what they want from an estate, but there is often more left over. Our stock is what remains."[1] This book addresses the historical value of the things families leave behind.

All family histories include stories, and often families have tools, clothing, souvenirs, photographs, letters, and so on that provide tangible evidence of both oft-told stories and other, perhaps untold, stories. The surviving materials can bring family stories alive for generations that didn't yet exist when the stories happened.

Family history isn't genealogy. Genealogy focuses on pedigrees, lineage, descendants, and so on—it focuses on who is related to whom and how. Genealogy provides the family tree that leafs out into a family's history. The accumulated belongings in the attic, closet, basement, garage, desk, and storage locker (hereafter referred to as "the attic"), contain the sap that feeds the leaves and flowers of the history of the individuals, families, and communities budding from that family tree.

Throughout most of our nation's history, families have passed household goods down through the generations as a form of both economic and emotional support. Giving and receiving a piece of furniture or a set of dishes helped a young couple get started in their own home. Giving and receiving a photograph album or a box of letters strengthened the bonds between the generations, especially when members of the younger generation moved away and out of easy communication with older ones. Those traditions began to change in the middle of the twentieth century.

After nearly two decades of the Great Depression and then World War II, the rising prosperity of the 1950s released a society-wide desire to purchase new and modern versions of nearly everything. Prosperity allowed young families to set up their homes without relying on the family hand-me-downs. Consequently, the post–World War II generation—the baby boomers—found themselves responsible for a vast accumulation of family belongings the prewar generation left behind. The boomers and their children (and others of their generations) now must make those keep-toss-donate decisions about the "stuff" they and their parents accumulated. It all serves as evidence in the story of individuals, of families, and of communities, but if a younger generation does not want the family's accumulated belongings, what happens to that family's historical evidence?

When a death occurs, friends and family members may clear out the family home without thinking of the family's historical legacy. As a result, the family and community history becomes fragmented, distorted, or lost because the complete story no longer exists in one place. Items with high monetary value may get sold. Unfortunately, when faced with artifacts and documents from relatives they don't remember, descendants find that hiring a dumpster or an auctioneer makes everything go away fairly easily.

We wrote *How to Weed Your Attic* for those facing the dilemma of what to do with the materials left behind. We want to help readers see the historical significance in the belongings handed down in their families. We use the term *historical significance* to denote an object's *usefulness for understanding the past*—things that illuminate a family's history, the history of the community in which the family lived, and even the greater world.

Learn to identify family belongings with historical significance.

We also hope this book will help professionals who assist families with financial or estate planning and other end-of-life decisions.

In the course of writing this book, we have discussed many of the ideas with other professionals, including the question of how much of a person's documentary history has historical value. Some argue that not everything has worth—address books came up as an example of something with a questionable value. Others argue that a researcher can find use for everything. An address book can help a historian or a genealogist create a network of friend and family connections, and it can provide specific information about exactly where people lived, thus providing a clue to their economic and social milieu. Address books don't usually have dates attached to the address (more's the pity), but at least they provide a usually sequential record of professional or domestic moves people make. Both authors have moved frequently—in the case of one of us, twenty-eight times since leaving college. Not every physical move created a different address, but most did.

Regardless of the differences of opinion among the professionals, for your purposes, assume that you will keep everything we don't explicitly say isn't worth keeping. If you ultimately decide to donate family papers to a repository, the professionals will make the final decision based on the mission of their collection; it doesn't have to be your problem.

The book addresses what you should keep for the sake of history in its largest sense. It does not discuss downsizing, although downsizing could result from following our suggestions. Similarly, this book does not discuss getting organized, although you might find yourself better organized if you follow some of our suggestions. Other authors have written about setting up family archives or preserving family artifacts, and we touch on those questions only tangentially. Here we aim at defining what materials contribute to our understanding of history and what to do if you don't want to or can't keep them. We focus on how family artifacts and documents can contribute to a larger understanding of the world—especially if they become part of a historical repository's collection.

Admittedly, both authors have a fondness for repositories; we've spent most of our careers working in and around them. Elizabeth has focused on archival repositories, and Lucinda has worked in both museums and archives. We have both moved many times, and we have both cleaned out our parents' homes after their deaths. The idea for the book grew out of our awareness of the confusion that a thousand little decisions can cause as you decide, one item at a time, what to do with a house full of family belongings. It also came from our distress at how much historically valuable evidence goes to the dump. We know that shows like the popular *Antiques Road Show* can instill a fear of ignorance of the market value of old items as watchers see a participant's one-dollar yard sale purchase receive an estimated value in the hundreds or thousands of dollars. We assume that a similar fear of ignorance of historical value also lurks within many readers, but we know that if you use this book your understanding of what constitutes historical value will increase and you will gain confidence about sorting your family's belongings.

HOW TO USE THIS BOOK

When you address the generational accumulation of your family, you confront these two questions, among many others:

1. What should we keep because it has historical significance?
2. What should we do with what we keep?

To address Question 1, we started the book with a general discussion of historical value. We then divide attic residue into four categories: (1) mass-produced, (2) handmade or custom-made for an individual person, (3) business-related, or (4) commemorative materials. In each category, we organize the types of materials alphabetically—address books, diaries, homemaking equipment, musical instruments, and so on. In the descriptions, we do not define the items. We assume you know what they are, and we simply make a straightforward assessment of their potential historical value and, in case you might not want to keep them, how an archive or museum might look on them. We do not comment on collectible value, although many items of historic significance also have value as collectibles. Nor do we comment on monetary value, though historically valuable materials often have monetary value.

The last three chapters address Question 2—what to consider after you have decided what's worth keeping for historical purposes. Chapter 7, "Special Issues," explains the need to establish clear ownership, the best way to handle privacy matters, the existence of legal restrictions on certain items, and other issues. For those of you who want to keep your historically valuable items, in chapter 8 we include very basic guidance on how to take care of them, and we point you to many more detailed sources of information. For those of you who cannot keep your items with historical value, in chapter 9 we provide a basic road map for donating them to a repository.

We do not expect you to read this book from cover to cover. Rather, think of it as a cross between a guidebook and a reference book. Read chapters 1, 2, and 7–9 now, for guidance, and turn to chapters 3–6 for reference when you start confronting the contents of your attic.

NOTE

1. Reil Nason, *All the Things We Leave Behind* (Fredericton, NB: Goose Lane Editions, 2016).

1

Why Things in
Your Attic Matter to History

We all wonder about the past and what it was *really* like. David Lowenthal, who has written extensively on why and how we long to understand the past,[1] shows how, as part of our wondering, we cling to painfully or joyfully vivid memories of events we experienced and to nostalgic recollections of times and events we've only heard or read about. We even embrace an idealized past we've created from all we've experienced, heard, and/or read. Lowenthal makes clear that we cannot ever truly know the past, so we hold fast to things from the past, trying to absorb all the information and evidence they can provide. We do this as individuals and as societies. Historians and anthropologists spend their careers trying to make sense of the past by studying the objects and written materials our ancestors left behind.

Before the 1960s, formal historical research focused primarily on large political events and powerful people from the past—wars, kings, queens, presidents, and revolutions. Museums and archives of the time collected great art, the papers of the movers and shakers of society, and the tangible evidence of greatness. This practice began to change in the 1960s and 1970s because of broad political and social upheavals brought about by the civil rights movement, the student movement, the women's movement, the environmental movement, the struggle against the war in Vietnam, and so on. These social events spawned new ways of looking at history and new assumptions about its study. Historical research became less focused on the great and powerful and more directed toward the lives of ordinary people. Researchers delved into social history with all of its subsets—labor history, family history, rural history, urban history, industrial history, and so on—dividing all those topics by ethnicity, race, class, and gender. In a way and to an extent that had not happened previously, historians looked to material culture—clothing, furniture, tools, and toys—and to common documents—advertising, ephemera, local archives, postcards, and newspapers—to understand the events of the past from many points of view. Museums and archives have adapted to these broad cultural developments and the number of cultural institutions devoted to history has increased. What they collect and how they display and interpret their collections has also changed.

Cultural institutions—museums, archives, historical societies, historic houses, libraries art galleries and so on—guard our historical evidence. They collect, organize, preserve, and make historical and socially important materials available to audiences of all ages and depths of interest. Since the 1990s, the number of cultural institutions devoted to history of all types has more than doubled. Cultural institutions devoted solely to history or general topics now make up almost 90 percent of all museums in the United States, while art museums represent only 4.5 percent.[2] With the increasing emphasis on history, items that museums would once have spurned as too trivial have become items of historical interest. Since the 1960s, documents like diaries and correspondence of obscure people have interested researchers who see them as valuable historical evidence. In the past, researchers looked on photographs as merely supporting documentation for other, more important, papers. Now researchers see them as valuable sources of information in their own right.

These changes in our cultural understanding and the study of history play a central role as we consider the significance of the objects and papers we find in the family attic. The changes sharply increase the significance of family collections as sources of historical information that have importance beyond the family circle. This historical significance makes it desirable for families to consider placing their collections in historical repositories that will preserve them for future generations of researchers.

The objects we save year after year often denote special or notable events or times or people in our lives or the lives of our family members: a braided rug your grandmother made, your last Christmas doll, the crocheted place mats your parents received as a wedding present, your children's sports' trophies, the baby shoes your grandmother wore on the boat when her family immigrated to America, your father's war medals, a rolling pin used by your maternal great grandmother, your wedding dress, your grandfather's favorite chair. These objects, along with the stories that accompany them, can tell us about the context and content of our lives, our families, and the wider community. And they can provide valuable clues for historians studying a community or period of time.

Further, advertising flyers, movie tickets, greeting cards, packages and bags from stores, even buttons with advertisements, sayings, or political topics convey a great deal of information about the person who owned them, their community, and their lives. The creators of this ephemera, meant it for temporary use, assuming it would not survive the event.

When it does survive, it becomes tangible and valuable evidence of history.

Personal and family documents work in a similar way. We build our understanding of a time or place or group using a scaffolding of personal records—birth, school, marriage, death, letters, diaries, financial records—and public records such as news accounts, government records, and organizational records. Preserving documents assures that evidence of essential activities in our lives and the lives of our communities is carried forward accurately and adequately. Preserving historical evidence requires preserving a wide range of documents that validate our personal and group identities and histories.

Legal documents track our obligations and our commitments, so we routinely keep contracts, wills, and other legal documents for use by this generation, and perhaps generations that follow. Other legal records, such as land records, probate records, and divorce settlements track our property ownership. Housing records explain the infrastructure of our lives—our homes and the contents thereof. Finally, financial documents chronicle our financial obligations and relationships.

As personal and family records clarify the relationships of individuals and groups to the rest of the world, organizational records reveal the operation of organizations—including commercial, recreational, political, and charitable—that we participate in. They clarify the networks among people and organizations that facilitate and influence the lives of communities.

Collectively, our records document the waxing and waning of community, organizations, family, and personal lives. They embody and reflect the accumulated wisdom, aesthetics, and experience of our civilization. Without them, we would have only our immediate memory, trapping us in the limbo of the present. Documents and objects provide the evidence we need to understand our social institutions, the human condition, and the events that arise from both. Documents and objects tell us how things work and how things came to be as they are.

Family objects and archives inform us about our ancestral past and inform our future. They survive as palpable evidence of the past, and they can help us avoid falling into the trap of nostalgia. Personal stories often make the most compelling history. Consider the difference between a movie version of the settling of a frontier compared to the letters and diaries of people who actually settled it. Objects and archives reveal the difference between the myth and the reality of the growth and melding, or not melding, of the many people and cultures that created the United States.

Family collections enlighten our understanding of the past; they have important lessons to impart to the wider world. Every family has items that tell the story of what is important to and about a family. However, over time, their significance within a family dwindles. A cache of letters from the old country may have great meaning as long as family members remember the writers and can read the letters written in a different language from the one they speak. After the memories of the people or the linguistic access disappear, the ties to the correspondence within the family circle may dwindle to nothing, *but its significance to the history of the wider community will not.*

The historical significance of many documents never disappears.

Family collections include the memorabilia that belonged to the individuals of the family and community and that relate to the resources, values, causes, and activities that created and influenced their history. By donating them to a historical repository, you can treat materials that formerly had significance for the family or a family member in a way that honors the family without burdening future generations with the overwhelming task of preserving things that no longer mean anything to them.

Prudence had a conversation with her first cousin, Ted, about their mutual grandfather. Ted had acquired the grandfather's papers and had written a biography of him. He suggested to Prudence that since he had written the grandfather's biography, he could probably throw the papers away. Shock ran through Prudence's body. NO! Ted had used the papers to examine what interested him about their grandfather—his success as a businessman. Prudence wanted to see what she could find in the papers about his many civic activities. She pointed out to Ted that he had interpreted their grandfather one way; she wanted to know more about him another way. She suggested Ted donate the papers to a repository so many researchers could understand their grandfather's life in many different ways.

Caveat! Even when something has no historical significance, it may have sentimental value, although many items have both. When you discover things with a lot of sentimental value but no historical value (an old high school diploma, a dried-up corsage, or a souvenir scarf from the Horseshoe Curve, for example), keep them until you're really ready to throw them away. *Never throw away or give away anything until you're emotionally ready.* Once it's gone, it's gone—probably forever.

When Mary's husband died, she confronted their newly occupied still-overcrowded retirement house full of stuff. She and David had married in late middle-age, and much of David's stuff came from his life before her. Professionally he had gained international prominence in his career, and Mary recognized that his files and computers contained important material that belonged in a repository, available to anyone interested in David or the early years of the discipline he had helped develop. She made arrangements with the Special Collections Department of the university where he had taught, which happily received his professional papers and computers.

David also had a lot of material from his ancestors, and they meant nothing to Mary. She gave it all to his children from a previous marriage. That left the personal and professional materials from their life together. It took Mary longer to part with them, but as time passed and her grief abated, she recognized what belonged at the university and what belonged with his children, and she passed them along. Some things, however, so fully represent her very happy life with David that she may never part with them.

RESOURCES

Culbertson, Judi, and Marj Decker. 2005. *Scaling Down: Living Large in a Smaller Space*. Emmaus, PA: Rodale. A book that focuses on how to simplify your life, control clutter, and pare down your possessions for a move into smaller living quarters.

Dellaquila, Vickie. 2017. *Don't Toss My Memories in the Trash. A Step-by-Step Guide to Helping Seniors Downsize, Organize, and Move*. Second edition. Self-published. Written by a professional organizer with a background in health care and social services, this book addresses the logistical and emotional aspects seniors face about housing—moving versus aging in place, different types of retirement living, health and financial considerations that appear everywhere, and what to do with their possessions.

Fleming, Ann Carter. 2004. *The Organized Family Historian: How to File, Manage, and Protect Your Genealogical Research and Heirlooms*. Nashville, TN: Rutledge Hill. The book provides instructions on organizing family history files, family interviews, photographs, and heirlooms.

Hall, Julie. 2007. *The Boomer Burden: Dealing with Your Parents' Lifetime of Accumulation of Stuff*. Nashville, TN: Thomas Nelson. Pragmatic advice on facing your parents' death, managing the things they leave behind, and the family dynamics that may arise.

Mannon, Melissa. 2011. *The Unofficial Family Archivist: A Guide to Creating and Maintaining Family Papers, Photographs, and Memorabilia*. Self-published. A guide to the care of personal papers, photographs, and memorabilia, written for people who want to preserve their family history.

Rinker, Harry L. 2007. *Sell, Keep or Toss? How to Downsize a Home, Settle an Estate, and Appraise Personal Property*. New York: House of Collectibles. Practical advice on how to simplify the complicated personal, familial, and financial decisions involved in cleaning out a house.

NOTES

1. David Lowenthal, *The Heritage Crusade and the Spoils of History* (Cambridge: Cambridge University Press, 1997); David Lowenthal, *The Past Is a Foreign Country* (Cambridge: Cambridge University Press, 1985).

2. Institute of Museum and Library Services (IMLS), "Government Doubles Official Estimate: There Are 35,000 Active Museums in the US," IMLS News Release, May 19, 2014.

2

General Rules for Making Decisions

Discerning whether something has historic value amounts to following a fairly simple set of rules:

1. A complete or long collection has more value than a partial one.
2. Emotive material provides a richer picture than factual material.
3. Unique usually has more value than mass-produced, but not always.
4. Documents and objects carry information beyond what the sender intended.
5. A twenty-five-year rule exists without our consciously knowing about it.

We explain them below.

1. A COMPLETE OR LONG COLLECTION
HAS MORE VALUE THAN A PARTIAL COLLECTION

For purposes of historical understanding, one school report card piques our interest; a whole set reveals a child's strengths, weaknesses, and academic growth. Similarly, one letter written by your ancestor describing his experiences working at a winter resort doesn't provide as much historical information as the set of letters he wrote over the entire season.

Similarly, incomplete objects do not carry as much significance as complete ones. A handle from an eighteenth-century farm tool doesn't tell us as much as the complete tool. Regardless of objects' signs of wear and age, if they have all their parts, you can consider them complete. They do not need to function as they did originally. If, on the other hand, an object made up of many parts has lost some or most of them, the remaining parts may have value, but the significance of the whole object has diminished substantially.

The diaries of C. D. Earl.
Collection of Henry Sheldon Museum of Vermont History, Middlebury, Vermont.

The diaries of C. D. Earl, a traveling salesman who sold hardware, cover 1853 and 1862–1897. Earl started his career in the late 1850s by selling for the Fairbanks Scale Company in St. Johnsbury, Vermont. For the next thirty years, he traveled throughout northwestern Vermont and northeastern New York State. Between 1868 and 1879, he partnered in the hardware business with several people in Middlebury, but he continued to travel. Mr. Earl used his diary to record the territory he covered each day, where he stayed, what he paid for anything he bought, and the essential details of business deals he made. Individually the diaries are really boring, but because there is such a long run of diaries, researchers can use Earl's record to document people, prices, business practices, and the growth of communities. We watch his business grow, the accommodations that he was able to find in various places change, the markets and product lines evolve with technology, and the communities on his route develop.

Dr. Poole worked for the Tennessee State Department of Education during the 1950s, traveling through rural areas helping to place children in appropriate schools. He specialized in the emerging field of child psychology, and he used the Revised Stanford-Binet Scale, a standardized test to measure the attention, memory, and verbal skills of schoolchildren and, thereby, their intelligence. The test kit itself came in a carrying case that held its many different parts: directional pamphlets, artwork, drawings, blocks, dolls, toys, and other manipulatible devices. Eventually, Dr. Poole became a college professor and his Stanford-Binet test kit and all of its contents were relegated to the attic. Dr. Poole's children found it and loved playing with the blocks and toys and using the drawings for paper drawings of their own. Eventually the toys broke or were lost, the pamphlets and papers thrown in the trash, and only the case with its empty compartments remained. The significance of the kit, the stories it could have triggered, and the information it conveyed completely disappeared with its missing parts.

2. EMOTIVE MATERIAL PROVIDES
A RICHER PICTURE THAN STRICTLY FACTUAL MATERIAL

In a hundred years, historians and biographers will have difficulty writing a very personal biography of a person in the late twentieth century. Today we all have complicated and well-documented business lives—we have financial documents coming out our ears—but rarely do we sit down and write thank you notes, much less long letters or diaries. If we need to reveal our deepest concerns or confess our heartfelt feelings, we do it over the telephone or through email or texting rather than through some more permanent medium like paper.

James M. Slade, a prominent Vermont lawyer and politician, served in a number of state and national offices, and he kept diaries. His ten diaries cover 1861, 1863–1865, 1868–1871, and 1874–1875. As a public person, James Slade interacted with and commented on events in the wider world more than most small-town diarists. He also made more personal notes about his family life than most male diarists. His son and daughter-in-law lived in his household, and on February 19, 1871, he noted, "My precious Grandson is very sick and I am severely afraid he mite never get well." Thereafter, almost daily, he noted his other business, and then commented on the baby's health. For example, "February 21: 'At work on accounts. Bro __?__ from Brandon preaching this evening. Baby boy quite ill.'" He did this daily, until April 8, when the baby finally died. Today, that child would have gone to a hospital and likely survived. In a way that no third-party account could impart, these cryptic notes reveal the relentless stress around life and death before modern medicine.

While many people kept diaries—short factual accounts of daily activities—others kept journals. Journals usually hold longer entries that observe or reflect on daily activities. While diaries frequently did not contain a lot of emotion, journals frequently do.

The journal of Mary Ann Swift.
Collection of Henry Sheldon Museum of Vermont History, Middlebury, Vermont.

Mary Ann Swift, a young woman about whom we know little beyond her membership in a prominent family, kept journals from 1862 to 1865. Mary Ann wrote out her soul in her journal, beginning on June 1, 1862. In August, her brother died during the Peninsula Campaign of the Civil War, and she mourned deeply. As she did, she wrote about her family's gratitude at having his body returned. She understood keenly that many families would never see their fallen loved ones again, because the government had no organized way to retrieve casualties from the battlefield. Instead, some local group buried them in a mass grave near the battlefield as the rush of war continued on (Faust, 2008). Mary Ann also wrote about the local historical society and how one of the local movers and shakers became outraged when he learned that the Vermont Historical Society announced its plan to hold its annual meeting in Middlebury without even asking him! Even though Mary Ann Swift's journals cover only four years, they provide rich detail and insight into her life and community that exists no place else.

The dozen surviving journals kept by Sedgwich W. Bidwell, a Methodist minister, span 1849–1887. Bidwell poured out his soul on a daily basis. He judged his a hard life. In fact, he suffered many losses and setbacks, but no more than most people at the time. The way he looked at his life, however, made his a hard one.

C. D. Earl's diaries, because twenty-five years of them survive, give us insight into the growth of a region, but not the man. Mary Ann Swift's journals, despite the fact that only four years exist, give us deep insight into one young woman and the world through her eyes, but they include only what touched her emotionally. Sedgwich Bidwell's incomplete set of journals reveal how his life and community evolved, and how his perspective influenced his experience of life.[1] Though none of these diaries and journals paints a complete picture of the creator's life, we know more about Earl, Swift, and Bidwell than future generations will know about their twentieth-century counterparts, because of the medium on which they stored their memories. Therefore, the diaries and journals have become valuable historical documents, even though (or perhaps because) the people who wrote them lived fairly ordinary lives. In addition, a researcher might find something in one that adds to something recorded in others.

Without documents like these, we would have little insight into the details and rhythms of life in that time and place. With them, and many others, we get some understanding of how people lived and how they played their roles in their families and communities. Through them we can get some understanding of how daily life and the community have changed, or not changed, to get us to the world we live in today.

Andrea's work on her Kentucky family genealogy at the Library of Congress serendipitously led her to a collection containing a journal and valuable information about a family member in a neighboring town. The journal, correspondence, and other papers shed valuable insight into her relative's mining community during the 1930s. The diary details the efforts of volunteers from a Quaker organization working at a mining camp in Letcher County, Kentucky, to improve social conditions for the inhabitants of the area. Andrea was thrilled to find out more about individual members of her family and information about their daily lives, their work, and the community in which they lived—all because she visited a large repository full of archival materials.

3. UNIQUE HAS MORE SIGNIFICANCE THAN MASS-PRODUCED

In the world of archives, nothing trumps something handwritten. Handwriting carries the perceptions and opinions of the writer in the moment of writing; its uniqueness makes it valuable. By the same token, today many people compose personal messages on a computer that they then print out like a mass-produced publication, such as Christmas letters sent to family and friends. All such letters have some value because they carry personal information and perspectives, and they do not have so wide a distribution to qualify as mass-produced documents. But, the personalized note the sender adds to the letter makes it unique, and eminently worth keeping.

Objects may have more value when made by hand, but not always. At one time, most objects were made by hand, either at home or by artisans trained to make furniture, pots, shoes, and so on. We identify handmade goods by the maker, workshop, or by a tradition of makers. Examples of such goods can be of great value to your family or your community if you can identify the maker or workshop.

With the onset of the Industrial Revolution, however, more and more goods came from factories. Common mass-produced objects do not have

Handwritten documents carry unique personal information and perspectives, which make them valuable.

much historical value because we can find a duplicate relatively easily, *unless they have great stories.* A mass-produced toy, if once owned by a child celebrity, for instance, would interest a museum that collects that sort of thing.

Mass-produced objects may have more value than handmade objects if they are rare, if they represent a company no longer in business, or if they are peculiar to a place. Much depends on condition and individual considerations as to place and type of object. If your grandmother kept her handmade dress from the 1930s, it might now represent something historical. Fortunately, if she kept one dress, she probably kept others from ensuing years. If they were in good condition and represented typical fashion designers during the decades 1940s–2000s, they would serve as examples of changing styles and popular culture.

4. OBJECTS AND DOCUMENTS CARRY INFORMATION BEYOND THE INTENDED

Everything you handle carries the information that the creator intended, but it also carries other information. Look for that as well. For instance, most people get a bill from a credit card company every month. The company sends the bill to explain how much the card holder owes, but in the process the bill provides a good record of the card holder's spending habits, implying the amount of discretionary money the card holder thinks he or she has, plus consumer tastes, priorities for spending money, and so on.

This photograph of a family posed on the porch of the Vance Bros. General Store in Paducah, KY shows not only a building no longer standing and its details, but their means of transportation.

The backgrounds of pictures also carry unintended information. The photographer intended to capture the image of a group of cousins at a family reunion—cousins you no longer recognize—but in the background the image of the family house and barn shows how the homestead looked at the time, which only vaguely resembles how it looks today. Pay attention and notice the hidden stories as you decide whether or not to keep something.

Unlike documents, objects generally carry almost no meaning by themselves. They need the stories that surround them, and they may reveal parts of their stories only to an expert eye. For instance, someone trained and knowledgeable about furniture would be able to identify furniture made in a particular time or place or by a particular maker. Family

Objects need the stories behind them to be historically significant.

objects will retain their meaning only as long as their stories stay with them. Record the stories that go with your materials so you do not lose the meaning of an object or set of documents. Get as much story as you possibly can.

Ann's memory of her grandmother's New York apartment always included the old trunk. Perfectly restored, it sat against a wall in the living room. No one in Ann's family spoke much about their history, but she did know her grandmother had emigrated from eastern Poland to America after World War II. While the family sorted the grandmother's belongings, Ann's father explained that the trunk was the only thing that survived the family's journey of exile from Poland to the United States during the chaos of the last days of World War II and the early days of the Communist takeover of Poland. It had carried everything the family could rescue, from the clothes they needed to family photographs, as they followed liberating forces across Europe and eventually to America. Instead of being just another piece of furniture, as Ann had always assumed, the trunk represented her family's Polish heritage and its epic World War II history.

Some documents read more easily than others. For instance, a budget with accompanying income and spending records tells a significant story about how the budgeters managed their life. The budget record tells what they did with their money—how much they paid for housing, what they paid for transportation, where they shopped, what they ate. It provides an indication of how much discretionary income they had. A collection of budget books or financial ledgers kept over a number of years will tell a researcher a great deal about the person who kept them. But to get that information, the researcher must do a fair amount of calculating and manipulation. The same holds true for the financial records that businesses keep.

Middlebury, Vermont, has an extraordinary collection of late eighteenth-century and early nineteenth-century ledgers housed in the Henry Sheldon Museum of Vermont History. By linking transactions in the ledgers, we can see how frontier Middlebury grew and the economic interconnectedness that made it viable. As the merchants kept their ledgers, they did not think, "Two hundred years from now those who want to know about the founding of Middlebury will find my ledger very useful!" They kept them as a way of keeping track of who owed them money and whom they owed. Today, the records provide significant historical insight.

Even personal letters and diaries can present puzzles that someone will need to sort out. The writers assume the reader knows the backstory for everything that gets mentioned. Descendants and historians will need to do at least some research to genuinely understand the contents.

While Genny researched her family tree, she collected all the papers, letters, stories, and photographs she could from her living relatives. She did well in tracing Irish roots on her father's side and Scottish on her mother's. Her aunt had given her a box of papers pertaining to her great-great-grandfather, Joshua, who was an enigma. The box contained a handwritten receipt for $7.50 made out to the "Home for the Friendless" for a train fare from New York City to Chicago in 1858. The box also held a cloth fragment embroidered with initials "JWK," several letters from Genny's great-great-grandmother to Joshua from the late 1870s, and advertisements for the Avery Company in Peoria, Illinois. What did all these clues mean? Could more research reveal what the "Home for the Friendless" did and why Joshua might have a receipt for that train ticket? Whose initials were those on the cloth fragment? Why did Joshua keep the Avery Company advertisements?

Sometimes documents can present puzzles that require research to sort out.

5. A TWENTY-FIVE-YEAR RULE EXISTS
WITHOUT OUR CONSCIOUSLY KNOWING ABOUT IT

We acquire objects and documents, use them until we no longer need them, and then we put them aside. If they go to the attic, they could sit there for decades. If they survive for about twenty-five years, or about one generation, they will become relics of the previous generation or age, and we will look at them with new eyes. We will see them as historic relics and may actively seek to preserve them.

An object that sits in the attic for twenty-five years or more, may become historically significant because it survived.

Wendy received a state-of-the-art portable radio on her fifteenth birthday in 1958. She used it through high school and college, lugging all six pounds of it everywhere she went. By the time she started teaching, portable radios had become much smaller, so she replaced it. The old one evoked too many memories to just discard, so Wendy put it in her parents' attic, where it sat for the next few decades. By the time she rediscovered it, she had passed age fifty and it had passed thirty-five. It amazed her children as an example of early portable radios, so rather than just being an old radio, it had become a remnant of her past, a relic of old technology—a historical object.

If you find it hard to see historical value in something that went to the attic just last year, assume everything has lived in the attic for at least thirty years, and look on it as old. Then decide if it has any historic value.

NOTE

1. Charles D. Earl's diaries, Mary Ann Swift's journal, and Sedgwich W. Bidwell's diaries, and James W. Slade's diaries are housed at the Henry Sheldon Museum of Vermont History, Middlebury, Vt.

3

Historical Value: Mass-Produced Material

When it comes to mass-produced objects and documents, both museums and archives want representative samples—not complete collections. They want enough to show how design, materials, and function or use changed over time for any type of object (e.g., telephones) or document (e.g., high school diplomas). They do not want a large collection. If the repository collects only local material, it will not want objects from afar. After repositories have what they want, they might accept a replacement in better condition, but they won't want to add more just for the sake of having more. If you offer a repository something, the acquisitions people will look closely for the right mixture of condition, age, provenance, completeness, and available space at a repository—we've abbreviated the concept of those collective qualities as CAPCAS.

Condition refers to how little damage an item has suffered; the less damage, the better. Age generally means the older the better, but it can mean something from a specific time. Provenance refers to the history of who owned or used the item over its lifetime. Items owned and/or used by important people have more historical value than those owned or used by nobody in particular. Completeness refers to whether all the parts and pieces remain with the item—a hotel register with all its pages or a tool with all its parts. Finally, the repository will assess whether it has Available Space to store responsibly the item you're offering.

EVALUATION OF MASS-PRODUCED ITEMS

Here we list the wide range of mass-produced objects and documents, and give a one-word evaluation for the historical value of them. We use the scale "Always, Usually, Maybe, Rarely, Never" to evaluate historical significance; the description also adds more detail. We add the phrase "CAPCAS applies" to indicate how a repository will assess something from this category if you offer it to its collection.

Advertising Premiums and Ephemera—Usually

Key chains, pens, and kitchen gadgets that businesses gave away show how businesses presented themselves to customers and potential customers. Advertising ephemera usually has historical significance as a record of local business. Further, advertising premiums often reflect design trends and have value for the study of the evolution of design and typography. CAPCAS applies.

Books—Rarely

Libraries collect books, so discarding a book will not destroy a valuable historical resource. However, if you have old books of particular local interest—a local topic or written by a local author—it may have research value to your local library or historical society. Otherwise, as a general rule, most of what you have falls under the heading of old books, not rare or valuable books. To get a sense of the value of a book, look it up on Addall (www.addall.com) or talk to an antiquarian bookseller. (See also "Libraries" in chapter 4.)

China, Dishes, and Glassware—Maybe

Many families have several generations of dishes but few members that want them. These sets of china might interest a museum. Some museums use donated china and tea sets at events; they may also use them as display props or in educational programs. CAPCAS applies.

Clothing—Maybe

All clothing carries stories, and, depending on the story, it may have historical significance, especially the following common types of store-bought clothing and accessories. If you have clothing, get the stories that go with it. CAPCAS applies.

Accessories: Hats, handbags, purses, belts, gloves, stockings, collars, shoes, scarves, and other accessories to clothing may be important historically if they are associated with a notable local individual, were made locally, or were associated with an outfit. They may also interest a collecting institution to augment their clothing collection. Condition will matter to a repository, especially in the case of shoes and hats, which tend to be made of organic materials and receive a great deal of wear. Older hats with feathers may also fall under the Migratory Bird Treaty Act of 1918. (See chapter 7.)

This collection of china would get evaluated from many angles before acquisition into a historical repository.

Occupational Clothing and Uniforms: Ordinary work clothes may have particular historical significance because most examples were used until they were worn out and discarded. Thus, regardless of condition, occupational clothing and uniforms might interest a historical society. Some general stores sold manufactured clothing under their own label. Examples of those might interest a local museum as representative of the businesses in the community.

Military uniforms represent historical events, but any particular uniform doesn't usually carry much history alone. Battle medals, ribbons, and other decorations mark the specific places and military movements in which an individual wearing the uniform was involved, but the actual story behind the decorations may have died with the service-man or -woman who earned them. Because they can't bear to throw military wearables out, families often save them, but eventually want to give them to a local museum. CAPCAS makes a big difference as the museum considers whether to accept the donation of military apparel.

School Uniforms may interest a local repository. CAPCAS applies.

If you have pictures that show your clothing being worn, or letters, or the sales receipts that describe the clothing, the documentation makes these bits of clothing stand out; keep it with the clothing. If you offer the cloth-ing to a repository, be sure to include the documentation.

Comic Books—Rarely

As a general rule, comic books are more collectible than historical, although some specialized museums and archives would welcome some comic books. For instance, very early comics from the nineteenth century have historical value, as do those issues that reflect the events and values of a particular time if they fit into a historical repository's mission. During World War II, pro-American characters became popu-lar, such as Captain America, a superhero created to aid the war effort. The first issue shows him in a costume of stars and stripes battling Adolf Hitler. An early proto-feminist figure, Wonder Woman first appeared in 1942, fighting for justice. Canada had its own comic book industry dur-ing World War II featuring an entire group of Canadian superheroes, such as Nelvana of the Northern Lights. Historians value these comics, now referred to as "Canadian Whites," highly. In 1963, the X-Men com-ics made their debut with a storyline created in part to address social issues of prejudice and persecution. Marvel introduced one of the first African American superheroes, the Falcon, in 1969. In 1970, amid the Vietnam and civil rights protests, DC Comics mirrored the social climate of the country by teaming up their conservative vigilante, the *Green Lan-tern*, with the left-leaning hero, the *Green Arrow*. Besides these widely distributed comics, those that fall outside the mainstream, focusing on anti-establishment political themes and printed in small batches—"underground comix" alternatives to restrictions placed on the industry by the Comics Code Authority—have historical value sought after by museums and archives.

Computers (Hardware)—Rarely

Most museums and archives cannot maintain old computer equipment and do not collect it, although a specialized museum of technology or computers might want specific examples of old technology. A more general museum or archives might use old electronic equipment as exhibit props or in its educational collection. In general, however, electronics have little historical value. They also have no practical value. If you can't use an electronic device, assume that archives, museums, schools, and public libraries can't either.

Computers (Software)—Rarely

Most repositories have no interest in vintage software unless they have a way to use it. (See also "Computer Hardware.")

Currency—Maybe

"Currency" includes paper money, coins, stock certificates, bonds, and stamps. If you find this type of material, first check to see whether it has any monetary value—does the company that issued the securities still exist? Is the money still used? Currency that has no monetary value may have historic value depending on its place of issue and its rarity. Archives or museums might use currency in teaching about geography or history or as display props. CAPCAS applies.

Ephemera—Maybe

The term *ephemera* refers to things designed to last for only a very brief time. Producers of junk mail, political or entertainment posters, political fliers, and so on expect that people will discard the materials after they have read them, and most people do. That means that items of ephemera that survive have some historical value, because they illuminate fleeting events that might otherwise go unnoticed. While ephemera usually refers only to paper documents, it can also include objects like packages, pillboxes, matchboxes, hatboxes, badges, buttons, ribbons (political and advertising), and give-away trinkets. CAPCAS applies.

During the Vietnam War, Senator George Akin of Vermont received an enormous amount of material related to protest or support for the war. His office staff filed it away, and when the Aiken papers went to Special Collections at the University of Vermont, the Vietnam era ephemera went as part of it. As a collection, filed in chronological order, it provides rich insight into the American debate over the Vietnam War. One piece might not mean much, but the full collection does.

However, even one piece of ephemera can sometimes cast a new light on our past history.

In the 1980s, Anne cleaned out an old outbuilding on her husband's family farm. During the late nineteenth century, her husband's grandfather had used the loft of one building as a sort of office, and his wastebasket had remained undisturbed for the better part of a century. In the wastebasket, she found a junk mail flyer, c. 1890, advertising rubber condoms available through the mail—clearly marked "For medicinal purposes only." That single piece of junk mail provides a detail of social history not widely known, making it an important historical document.

Farm and Ranch Equipment and Tools—Usually

Equipment and tools from farmers and ranchers, especially those in good condition and examples of older equipment or tools, generally have historical value, but CAPCAS makes a big difference.

Furniture—Maybe

Furniture may carry historical significance depending on its style, design, make or manufacture, ownership, condition, uniqueness or rarity, significance, quality, and other factors. Condition usually matters a great deal with manufactured pieces. Does the piece have its original finish with, perhaps, a patina showing wear from use? Has it been restored, painted, repaired, the hardware changed? If a local history repository wants a specific type of furniture or if it wants a piece belonging to a particular person or family, or if it wants something constructed locally, the decision makers will often overlook flaws in condition. Historical societies and museums may also need more ordinary or representative furniture for exhibit props or educational uses. Because of furniture's size, a museum will consider carefully whether it has adequate storage space. CAPCAS applies.

Furniture's historical significance depends on its style, design, make or manufacture, ownership, condition, uniqueness, significance, or quality.

After her mother died, Margaret had to settle the estate. Her mother had paid a great deal of money for some antique pieces twenty or more years ago, and she had told Margaret that they would bring a lot of money. When Margaret had an appraisal done of the furniture, all of the pieces appraised for less than the original purchase price. The appraiser explained that: (1) the current generation's interest in Victorian antiques had waned, (2) the demographic-driven death of large numbers of elderly had created an overflow of such antiques in the market, (3) the expansion of ways to procure antiques in the online retail world had caused prices for certain antiques to drop. Armed with this knowledge, Margaret donated the Victorian bed and table and several other pieces to the local house museum, which accepted them because they matched the time period and regional make called for in the museum's collection policy.

Games—Maybe

Commercial games can be historically significant because they reflect our culture and represent one of the oldest forms of human social interaction. Historical repositories will accept mass-produced games such as marbles, dominoes, card games, board games, video games, and modern electronic games if they have some tie to the locale, such as a company or person, or will serve to interpret a part of the repository's programs. Because games often come with various parts and pieces, wholeness and condition are essential acquisition points. CAPCAS applies.

Greeting Cards—Maybe

Cards make up a special category of art objects, because they reflect the world of commercial art and the sense of art and taste of an era and locale. Several museums, including the Smithsonian, systematically collect greeting cards; the Hallmark company has an archive of its cards. If you have *only* cards, do not worry about their historical significance, although a repository might accept a particularly rich collection to use as props in exhibits. CAPCAS applies.

On the other hand, every genealogist knows that cards provide evidence of a network of friends and family, making them historically valuable *if you can identify the sender and the recipient*. Other historical significance in family greeting cards lies in the personal notes that come with them; always keep the letters. If the sender wrote a letter or note on the card itself, keep the card.

Guns— Maybe

Manufactured guns and firearms may have historic significance, especially if they are older. If the gun happened to be manufactured locally, belonged to someone noteworthy, is rare or distinctive in some way, or has a connection with some identifiable and important event, a local repository may welcome it into its collections. If you own a firearm from one of the American wars or conflicts, perhaps a museum dedicated to that particular conflict would want it. However, laws govern the acquisition and ownership of firearms, and, as composite objects of both wood and metal in close contact, their condition and maintenance raises concerns. Safety and security also present problems, so local repositories respond cautiously and selectively when offered firearms. CAPCAS applies.

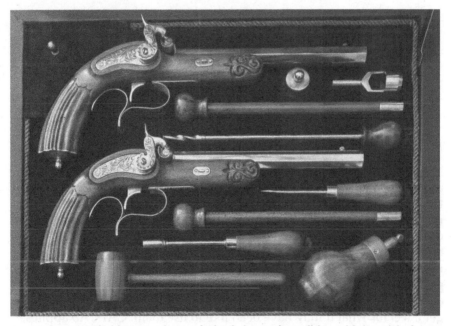

A complete set of older manufactured pistols in good condition with its original case and implements.

Be aware that antique guns may still hold live ammunition, and even after decades or hundreds of years, can be highly volatile and dangerous if they're loaded but not fired. As curator of museum collections with firearms, author Lucinda Cockrell saw loaded pistols from the 1840s, a Revolutionary War "Brown Bess" musket still loaded with buck and ball, a Civil War Springfield rifle complete with Minié ball, and even entire boxes of ammunition left at the museum door anonymously by metal-detecting enthusiasts. DO NOT try to unload a gun yourself; contact a museum objects conservator, professional gunsmith, or law enforcement official.

Holiday Decorations—Rarely

Families' holiday decorations may become family heirlooms, and they occasionally acquire value as historical objects. A collecting institution might use them for exhibit props, and as examples of artistic tastes and technology of their time. CAPCAS applies.

> A local history museum accepted the donation of a complete series of limited-edition Christmas ornaments representing historical buildings in the area. A local business had produced them for years, but many had not been available for decades. Because the donation was a complete set of locally produced ornaments depicting local history, the museum accepted them happily.

Homemaking Equipment—Maybe

The everyday implements for running a household tell us volumes about how the household preserved, prepared, and served food; cleaned the house; did the laundry; and so on. Household tools reflect cultural norms, and that gives them value as historical objects. Local historical societies may want some kitchen appliances reflecting changes across time, but, they have limited space for what they can accept. Some community museums welcome homemaking items for use in their educational programs. These "hands-on" classes are often held with school groups where children are allowed to work with utensils or at least handle the items to get a feel for what it may have been like to use them. CAPCAS applies.

> Margaret donated her family's spinning wheel to a local house museum. To the local Children's Discovery Museum, she gave an eggbeater, an iron, a butter churn, a butter mold, candy molds, and an iron cauldron.

Household Linens—Rarely

Most manufactured household linens have no historical value, unless they belonged to someone special or survived some major disaster. Some museums collect them as art or as exhibit props. Linens that have a local connection or something manufactured locally may interest a local historical society. CAPCAS applies.

Hunting, Fishing, Trapping Equipment—Maybe

Hunting, fishing, and trapping, once a necessity, have become pastimes. Equipment related to these activities might interest a museum if they reflect local customs or parts of the lives of important people. CAPCAS applies.

Jewelry—Maybe

Jewelry can interpret American fashion and other aspects of life, such as the economic practicalities of an era. For example, the stock market crash of 1929 and Great Depression made way for the growth of the costume jewelry industry, because people could no longer afford fine

Assorted jewelry with assorted historical significance.

jewelry. That era also opened the door for many immigrant jewelry craftsmen to emulate fine jewelry for affordable prices. Technological developments and the use of a new material called plastic "Bakelite" revolutionized manufacturing and made possible jewelry that was innovative, colorful, and inexpensive. Many local, regional, and national museums have such pieces of costume jewelry in their collections, especially as display props.

Jewelry associated with a particular maker, organization, or event might carry its own significance. Jewelry made in a traditional style, material, or technique from a particular place might also have an importance to local institutions. Finally, a piece of jewelry belonging to an important or specific local individual, especially if it is documented or tells a story, may be welcome to a historical collection. CAPCAS applies.

Knickknacks—Rarely

Most homes have trinkets and decorative knickknacks of all types—souvenirs from trips, bronzed baby shoes, novelty crafts, etcetera. Objects made locally or regionally may interest local history repositories; not much else will. CAPCAS applies.

Magazines—Rarely

Libraries all over the country keep a wide variety of magazines and journals; you don't need to.

Many a school librarian has reached the point of declining offers for *National Geographic* magazines. Some keep several sets: sets for cutting up, sets for art or geography projects, sets for checking out, and sets for use only in the library. After that, they simply don't have room for more. The same applies to *Life* magazines. If you have a long run of news magazines, *Time, Newsweek, Life, Look, Ebony*, etcetera, offer them to your local library, historical society, or high school, but don't feel rejected if they decline. If you can't stand to recycle them all, keep a sample—say all July and December issues—to show the change of fashion, tools, and concerns pertinent to the targeted audience.

If, on the other hand, you find stashed away somewhere the *Life* magazine edition that marked the end of World War II or an issue of the *Ladies Home Journal* from a date that carries no significance to you, keep it. A single issue says something about the person who saved it. He or she did not collect *Life* magazines for the sake of collecting *Life* magazines, so this particular issue must have contained something special—keep it as part of that person's papers where it might relate to other papers in the collection.

Musical Instruments — Rarely

Musical instruments that nobody plays anymore may or may not have historical significance. Instruments that belonged to and were played by a prominent local musician have more historical use than the beat-up plastic recorder played by all the kids in the family during their grade school years.

Many households will also have sheet music collections. Sheet music provides a unique window into American music and history, defining a time, event, war, social milieu, cultural trend, or human emotion. Sheet music published during a war period or some major event, promoting a dance craze, exposing stereotypes, fashions, advertising, singers, and such may have historical significance. CAPCAS applies.

In the middle of the twentieth century, greeting card manufacturers typically printed them on 8½" × 11" pieces of paper, which they then folded to create a front cover, back cover, and inside with their greeting and space for a short note. During the 1930s Depression years, when the people could little afford luxuries like sheet music, a company called Card Tunes printed sheet music on the back of the card's paper, in effect selling a card and a gift on one piece of paper.

Newspapers — Maybe

As with magazines, you can assume that some cultural institution nearby has a strong collection of any newspaper you might find. However, if you find very old newspapers—pre-1900—check with your local library, historical society, state archives, or an academic Special Collections Department or the Library of Congress to see if microfilm copies of the paper exist. If you have a run of a local paper, offer it to the local library or historical society as a source of issues to fill gaps in its collection. If you find only one or two issues that someone appears to have saved because of something special in it, keep it as part of the collector's papers.

Postcards — Always

Postcards have the potential for historical value in two ways—the image on one side, and the written content on the other. Commercially printed postcards became available by the mid-nineteenth century and

The postcard albums and postcards belonging to Glen's mother.

enjoyed wide popularity until the use of electronic media to send messages diminished their use.

Postcard paper for amateur photographers became available in the late nineteenth century, and people began creating their own photographic postcards. Those cards often contain images of places that have changed drastically, providing essential historical evidence not available in any other form. Further, many postcards document events from the creators' lives that they wanted to share with friends and family. Those images also have historical value. The message can provide a wide range of information from the mundane to the revelatory. Commercial postcards almost invariably document people's travel and activities. Either or both sides may have historical value, so keep postcards. They will interest the local historical repository of the locale they document.

Glen found two notebook albums of postcards in his mother's belongings while cleaning out her house. He noticed many of them were photographic images of houses or buildings in the small community he grew up in—buildings that no longer existed. A major interstate had been built years before, and the community store, church, and several houses had been torn down to make way for the highway. Glen also realized that the postcards were sent to his grandmother, aunts, and uncles from other family members and friends and dated from the early 1900s. The area's public library had a local history room and archive that was delighted to receive the postcard albums. Not only did the collection of real-photo postcards document a small community that no longer existed, but the comments on the cards also provided a snapshot into the lives of early twentieth-century women and farmers of the area.

Quilts—Maybe

(See "Household Linens.")

Religious Materials—Maybe

Archives and museums collect religious materials to document and interpret this important facet of human identity. Objects and materials associated with one of the nation's diverse religious faiths—Christian, Islamic, Jewish, Buddhist, Hindu, Native American, and others—include books, relics, music, musical instruments, furniture, documents, ceremonial objects, and art. Local repositories will prefer objects or materials with a local connection, person, event, or rarity. In addition, each religion has an archives or museum that focuses on its history. Groups, such as Shaker religious communities that thrived in the nineteenth century, have essentially died out. Much of their history and evidence of their practices and contribution to the larger culture lives in a variety of repositories. Other repositories focus on the dynamic role religious institutions played in African American communities during the nineteenth century, as well as the emergence of the modern civil rights movement. If your family was instrumental in the founding of your communities' church or religious affiliation, contact a repository. CAPCAS applies.

School Materials—Maybe

School materials, such as textbooks and school assignments, probably have no historical value, unless they have local importance. Materials representing education outside a formal classroom, such as materials from correspondence schools, might interest an archive if the materials have a local connection. CAPCAS applies.

Tools—Rarely

The term *tools* covers a range of objects. Here we refer to common mass-produced tools you will find in your home. Basic building and repair tools, automotive tools, kitchen implements, sewing tools, gardening tools, and such.

Mass production changed the world of tools by changing the design and variety of tools available. Most modern mass-produced tools do not have historical significance for a local museum or historical society. If you have older mass-produced tools of some sort, especially if they are now obsolete or unusual or have a definite local connection, they may interest a repository. CAPCAS applies.

Toys—Maybe

Mass-produced toys have more value as a collectible commodity than a historical one. They do, however, reflect the social and cultural values, events, and manufacturing methods of a certain time and place. Because of that, some historic house museums collect toys of a particular era to exhibit in period rooms, other repositories will seek popular and historically significant toys of a local nature, either manufactured locally or belonging to a well-known person. Specific manufacturers or types of toys are sought after by some museums depending on their collecting mission. For instance, a museum focusing on transportation might accept toy trains, cars, and airplanes. A local repository might want toys for their hands-on educational programs or exhibit props. The natural mix of children, play, and toys means toys usually show wear and tear and occasionally serious damage. Repositories usually only accept whole toys in good condition. CAPCAS applies.

A toy box full of mass-produced toys.

Vehicles — Maybe

Vehicles—that is, anything used to transport people or things from one place to another—appear in many museums around the nation and can hold great historical significance. Vehicles include wagons, stagecoaches, carriages, bicycles, motorcycles, cars, trucks, buses, trains, trams, trolleys, ships and boats, aircraft, and spacecraft. Almost every state has a museum dedicated to a particular make of automobile, motorcycle, boat, or other conveyance manufactured there. Local museums usually welcome old or rare vehicles that have a local connection. More modern vehicles associated with a particular event or local manufacturer, or bearing some distinction and in good condition may interest a repository. However, vehicles' large size and specialized technologies can present problems for exhibit, storage, and maintenance. CAPCAS applies.

Bob inherited the sleigh his grandfather used to deliver his foundry's furnaces and water-bath coolers to customers. Bob had always felt a special bond with his grandfather, and he cherished the sleigh as a symbol of that bond. Unfortunately, he had no place to store the 12' × 4' sleigh, so he arranged with the president of the local historical society to store it in the museum's storage space, although he retained full ownership. Quite active in the historical society, Bob kept a close eye on the sleigh, which, unfortunately, took up far more space than the historical society had to spare. When Bob died, none of his children wanted the sleigh, but a local collector did. Bob's children gave it to him, he moved it to his storage area, and the historical society regained valuable storage space. Everybody was happy.

Weapons, Other Than Guns—Sometimes

Weaponry such as swords, knives, and various bladed weapons, batons, clubs, shields, and bows and arrows may be important historically, especially if they have a connection with a particular event or significant person. Other significant components for historical acquisition include whether a weapon was locally manufactured, made by a skilled artisan, or bears some distinctive or rare markings, materials, components, or make. However, as with guns, safety and security present problems. Local repositories may respond cautiously and selectively when offered weapons. CAPCAS applies.

Danny's father fought in both the European and Pacific Theaters during World War II. He enlisted in the Navy in 1943 and participated in both the D-Day Normandy Invasion and the Battle of Okinawa. Like many servicemen of the time, he brought back "souvenirs" from the war when he received his honorable discharge in 1946. A Japanese officer's sword he picked up featured an ornate handle of ray skin. Through the years, Danny's father kept the sword in a closet, and brought it out periodically to be admired. Upon his father's death, the sword passed to Danny, who had always appreciated it and the war stories associated with it.

4

Historical Value: Individualized Material

Handwritten or handmade items usually have more historical value than mass-produced items. Typically, they reflect personal needs or tastes, or they show how people did what they needed or wanted to do before manufactured tools or toys made acquiring things easy. However, while archives will probably accept most of what you have to offer, after museums have examples of what they want, they might accept a replacement in better condition, but they won't want to add more to their collection just for the sake of having more. If you offer a repository something, the acquisitions people will look closely for the right mixture of condition, age, provenance, completeness, and available space at their repository—we've abbreviated the concept of those collective qualities as CAPCAS.

Condition refers to how little damage an item has suffered; the less damage, the better. *Age* generally means the older the better, but it can mean something from a specific time. *Provenance* refers to the history of who owned or used the item over its lifetime. Items owned and/or used by important people have more historical value than those owned or used by nobody in particular. *Completeness* refers to whether all the parts and pieces remain with the item—a hotel register with all its pages or a tool with all its moving parts. Finally, the repository will assess whether it has *Available Space* to store responsibly the item you're offering. A museum will apply CAPCAS criteria to handmade materials as readily as it will to manufactured goods.

EVALUATION OF INDIVIDUALIZED MATERIALS

Here, we list a wide range of handmade and individualized objects and documents, and give a one-word evaluation for the historical value of them. We use the scale "Always, Usually, Maybe, Rarely, Never" to evaluate historical significance; the description also adds more detail. We add the phrase "CAPCAS applies" to indicate how a repository will assess something from this category if you offer it to its collection.

Address Books—Always

Address books come in a variety of sizes and formats, but all have alphabetically organized spaces for names, addresses, and phone numbers of the entrants. Definitely keep them. They can have a lot of value for genealogists and local historians seeking to establish the networks, and, to some degree, the indisputable identity of people. An address book can help untangle people who may have identical or similar names. Address books also identify locations where people have lived. An address book someone used over several decades will track moves made by the people listed in it—frequently invaluable information one cannot acquire nearly as efficiently anywhere else.

Art Work—Usually

Although they aren't art museums, history museums, historical societies, and archives do contain works of art in their collections. Because the creation of art in various forms makes up an important part of our individual and collective lives, the paintings, sketches, prints, ceramics, pottery, art glass, sculpture, folk art, crafts, and such can have historical significance. Artworks created by noteworthy local artists, or of people, places, and events that no longer exist may be historically valuable. Folk art or works indicative of a specific area, people, or community provide historical evidence. History museums may have temporary exhibits of area artists. Some regions or towns with a thriving art scene will often have an active art and history museum in place with an ongoing display of local art. Most history museums will include an individual's art as part of a personal or family collection. Otherwise, CAPCAS applies.

Autograph Albums—Always

Autograph books catch people's thoughts, feelings, and perspectives. These sentiments can offer valuable insight into the tastes, interests, personalities, and concerns of individual compilers and their circle of friends and family as well as insight into the person doing the writing and his or her relationship and history with the owner of the book.

Birthday Books—Always

Sending birthday greetings serves to strengthen relationships among family and friends, and many people keep books designed to remind them of birthdays and anniversaries. Like address books, they provide clues to networks and help to distinguish between people with similar names.

Childhood Creations—Maybe

Works that children bring home from school, activity programs, athletic teams, and other groups they belong to frequently wind up in the parents' attics. The cleaner-out-of-the-attic should first offer them back to the creator, the true owner. Only when the owner declines, should the cleaner-out-of-the-attic proceed. Childhood materials' historical value depends in large measure on who created them, what they created, how well they did, how much the receiving institution might have of similar materials—in other words, CAPCAS applies.

At the end of his senior year in college in 1954, Ralph became engaged to his college sweetheart and then joined the army so he would have the GI Bill to help pay for graduate school. While he was stationed in Europe, Marilyn wrote him often. When he returned, they married and went off to graduate school. Ralph left many of his personal possessions at his parents' home, including Marilyn's letters, expecting he would retrieve them when they finished their schooling and had a permanent home. His mother, while cleaning out the attic, found the letters, decided they were nobody's business, and burned them. When Ralph, by then a historian, finally went to retrieve his personal belongings, he was shocked and disappointed, both as a person and as a historian, that they, his school report cards, high school and college notebooks, and all his childhood art no longer existed.

Clothing—Maybe

Clothing made at home, or made to order, or examples of work done by a particular dressmaker, tailor, or fashion house may interest a museum. CAPCAS applies.

During the Depression, certain feed companies recognized that many families could not afford to buy fabric to make new clothes for growing children or to replace worn-out clothing, nor could they create the special clothing that provides a sense of normal life, such as a new outfit at Easter. To compete for scarce money to buy flour, chicken feed, and so on, they began to package those products in brightly colored printed fabric that homemakers could use to make clothes. The Louisiana State University Textile and Costume Museum has a large collection of one family's clothing made from grain sacks.

If you also have documents that go with the clothing, the documentation makes the clothing stand out—photos give an overall feel of the people and times captured in the saved items of clothing. Any additional documentation, such as the pattern from which something was made, can also add to the garment's value. (See "Clothing" in chapter 3.)

Mary offered a high school prom gown to a textile museum. The curator hesitated until Mary explained that she had bought the dress from the spring 1959 Sears Roebuck Catalog. The museum had the catalog in its library collection, and the curator accepted the dress on the spot.

Commonplace Books—Always

Commonplace books hold every kind of information the owner might need: diary entries, financial notes, medical recipes, quotes, letters, poems, tables of weights and measures, proverbs, prayers, legal formulas, etc. Each commonplace book reflected its creator's particular interests, thus each has historical value.

Deeds—Probably

Deeds recording real estate transactions must be filed in a government office where, by law, the government must keep them forever. Therefore, if you have a copy of the deed given your ancestors when they bought their first property in America, you have a wonderful bit of family history, but the larger world does not need it to keep the historical record intact. That said, a repository some distance from the office holding the official record might want the real estate deed for the convenience of not having to send researchers to the official office, and it probably would want any other kind of deed.

Transfers of ownership of many types of property produce all sorts of deeds and can provide a wealth of historical information. Deeds can tell us about people long forgotten, family relationships, and more. They provide important land and urban history, showing agricultural, industrial, and residential development. Deeds can help research the history of a particular building or house and can portray changing property values. Deeds provide information about place names, street names that have changed, or places that no longer exist. They can show changes in local topography, such as building development, revised boundaries, strip mining, and farming. They may also show financial information in changing property values.

Good business practice involves keeping legal deeds. Older and rarer deeds may have historical significance. If you find a handwritten deed to a piece of land, a building, or something else from a past century, or if you think your document might be rare and not recorded, check with a local repository.

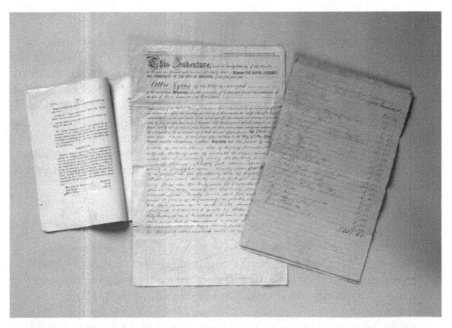

A deed for the sale of land in New York City dated 23 September 1843, along with other documents belonging to Albro Lyons.
From The New York Public Library, http://digitalcollections.nypl.org/items/510d47db-c58b-a3d9-e040-e00a18064a99.

Diaries—Always

If you have a long run of diaries or the diaries of a variety of writers who belonged to the same network of people, the diaries have great historical value. If you have a single diary that goes on at great length filled with opinions and observations about people and events—reasons why things are happening and what people thought—consider it a treasure. Even a simple diary recording only the weather can document a hurricane or a catastrophic unfolding event like long-term unemployment or a war.

The diary of Prudence, a young Massachusetts mill worker in 1843, records much the same news day after day: "—very hot, Did not go in," "—Went to work at 7 o'clock," "Still immured within the massy brick walls of a hateful factory." Prudence's entries tell us much and speak loudly of her situation, although they are not long or detailed.

Family Bibles—Rarely

In the nineteenth century, to which most family *Bibles* date, only a few companies produced these large volumes with pages designed for the recording of family membership and history. Most large genealogical societies have copies of all of printed versions, so the *Bible* part of the book has no particular historic value, but the genealogical information does. If you don't want to care for a book the size of a family *Bible*, remove the genealogical information and discard the book. If, however, you plan to give the book away, leave it intact and copy the genealogical information that interests you. If the book has some particular local interest, offer it to a historical society.

Zinck family descendants had several German-language family Bibles that their ancestors had brought from Germany in the 1840s. One family member had metal boxes made to protect them and found a scholar of old German to tell her about them. To her dismay, nobody in her children's generation cared to keep the *Bibles*, but the historical society in the county where the ancestors settled, and where some distant cousins still lived, received them happily.

Family Genealogies—Always

Family genealogies have great value to families and to local history organizations, as well as to genealogical libraries and archives. Genealogies that include more than just a chart listing of births and deaths have an even greater value. A repository may or may not want the research materials used to compile a genealogy. Since the Internet makes many primary documents available, the research documents may not add to your genealogy. However, not everything has reached the Internet and the research materials may have a general value—let the archivist decide what to keep.

Farm and Ranch Equipment and Tools—Usually

Handmade equipment and tools from farmers and ranchers, especially tools no longer used, have historical value. CAPCAS applies. (See "Farm and Ranch Equipment and Tools" in chapter 3.)

Home Movies and Videos—Always

Home movies and videos often contain documentation of subjects, places, events, even a former way of life. As a result, they hold historical significance to local historians, international scholars, and artists. Home movies come in a variety of formats and as one format succeeds another, the older becomes obsolete. Therefore, seek help in preserving your family films and migrating them from their current format to a widely held open-source format. Contact a historical repository for help. Many museums offer to reproduce home movies for the chance to preserve and document them in their collections and exhibits. Home Movie Day is an international event that invites people to bring their home movies to locations around the world to observe and celebrate these unique views of communities and cultures. Perhaps you can find one near you.[1]

A variety of home movie film and reels.

Steve's father took 8 mm film home movies of him during the 1960s while he was in the marching band in his hometown in Iowa. As the band marched down Main Street, Mr. Carpenter filmed the buildings, the crowd, and of course the parade itself. Fifty years later, silent 8 mm film showed color images of people no longer living and buildings no longer standing or drastically altered. Steve took the film to the university in town, and there the film/audio preservation department transferred the film to an open-source digital format. A copy went to the local historical society, which produced a special exhibit to interpret the changing face of Main Street over the past fifty years. The home movie was the star of the exhibit.

Homemaking Equipment — Usually

Handmade household tools reflect cultural norms, which gives them value as historical objects. CAPCAS applies.

Household Inventories — Always

Household inventories have enormous historical significance to both a family and a local museum or archives. Inventories describe what a family owned at a particular time, and several inventories over time allow us to draw inferences about the family's financial circumstances, social status, and personal aesthetics. They also allow us to trace how technological innovation spread though the general population.

On October 27, 1840, the home of Salisbury, Vermont farmer Samuel Sheldon, his wife, Sarah, and their nineteen-year-old son, Henry burned to the ground as the result of a fire in a nearby work shed. Samuel had fire insurance and submitted his claim with an inventory of goods lost in the fire.

"1 cook stove—5.00." Until a decade or so earlier, all cooking had been done in a fireplace. Sarah Sheldon had the latest in domestic technology in having a cook stove.

"1 box stove—2.00." Set in another part of the house for heat, the box stove probably was relatively new and much prized. The stoves were installed with "20 lengths pipe—7.50" and "6 elbows—8.00." The pipe was worth much more than the stoves.

The list indicates that the Sheldons had few luxuries. Except for the box stove, only "1 clock—1.00" might be considered a luxury. Domestic tools from Sarah's kitchen make up the bulk of the list: "1 Cake dish—.33; 1 Earthen pot—.30; 2 candlesticks—.33; Loom, etc.—7.00; 1 bureau—10.00; 7 runs woollen yarn—2.50; 1 pair pantaloons—3.00; 20 lbs. flax—2.25; 3 cupboards—10.00; 10 pr. stockings—3.00." The total came to $96.00. The family may have rescued beds, tables, and chairs, which do not appear in the inventory.

Sarah Sheldon had a modern stove, but she still did some, if not all, of her own weaving, despite the fact that twenty-five miles away in Middlebury, several textile mills provided cotton and woolen cloth to local stores. Apparently cooking in a fireplace vexed her more than weaving. While the fire disrupted the scheduling of the men's work and their domestic comfort, it destroyed Sarah's ability to do her work by destroying both her workspace and her tools. Further, by destroying her workplace and tools, it destroyed the rhythms and routines that may have provided her a sense of security and continuity with the past and present.

The family also lost its winter store of food: "700 bushels, Potatoes, 50 pounds clear pork in barrels, 30 pounds mutton, 25 bushels winter apples in barrels, 1/3 barrel soap, 1 bushel pickles, 40 bushels onions, 450 bushels corn in the cob equal to 225 bushels shelled corn, 2 bushels wheat."

Samuel either grew potatoes as a cash/barter crop or stored other's potatoes for them, so the loss of 700 lbs. of potatoes represented a substantial debt and/or loss of bartering power until the next potato harvest.

The insurance company refused to pay the claim on the grounds that Samuel had built the shed too close to the house. The Sheldons immediately put up a one-room cabin in which they lived while they rebuilt their home, completed in November 1841.

Household Linens—Maybe

When women made both clothing and household linens, including quilts, they frequently added fine embroidery, lace edging, insertions of all types, and other handwork. Commercial linens made or embellished by hand can show examples of the evolution of "women's work"; some have come to be recognized as an art form. Some museums collect them as art; others may use them as exhibit props. CAPCAS applies. (See "Household Linens" in chapter 3.)

A square from the 1904 quilt made of fair prize ribbons donated to the Henry Sheldon Museum of Vermont History.
Collection of Henry Sheldon Museum of Vermont History, Middlebury, Vermont.

The Sheldon Museum, in Middlebury, Vermont, recently received a 1904 handmade quilt constructed of sixteen individual "squares" that created a cover measuring 60" by 64." Each square consisted of an embroidered label with the initials of an exhibitor at a county fair and several award ribbons the exhibitor won, all set in a background of random, brightly colored pieces of cloth. An example of outstanding handwork, the quilt also documents decades of agricultural fairs that emerged during the nineteenth century's interest in scientific agriculture and created competitions for the "best" in many agricultural and domestic products. Interspersing competition ribbons from fair events and vibrant material, the crazy-quilt pattern brings together local tradition, sewing, quilting, and family history.

Hunting, Fishing, and Trapping Equipment—Maybe

Handmade hunting, fishing, and trapping equipment might interest a museum if it reflects local activities or customs or parts of the lives of important people. CAPCAS applies. (See "Hunting, Fishing, Trapping Equipment" in chapter 3.)

Jewelry—Maybe

Handmade jewelry associated with a particular maker, organization, or event might interest a museum. Likewise, jewelry made in a traditional style or technique might have importance to local institutions. (See "Jewelry" in chapter 3.)

Elizabeth's aunt, in her will, assigned Elizabeth the task of dispersing her jewelry. Elizabeth divided the modern pieces equitably among the family women per her aunt's wishes. Some older items puzzled Elizabeth. One looked like a pin or brooch of some kind, intricately woven from fibers into beads or balls then made into a knot with a small gold fitting engraved with the name "Lizzie." Elizabeth knew she had been named after her great-grandmother, also Elizabeth, but called Lizzie. She decided to take the brooch to a jeweler, and, to her amazement, she learned it was made of human hair. During the Victorian era, and earlier, the hair of beloved friends and relatives was hand-braided or woven into bracelets, chains, rings, earrings, and more and worn as treasured mementos or memorialized as mourning jewelry. Elizabeth's hair-work brooch was no doubt made from her great-grandmother's hair, perhaps by another family member. The town's history museum readily accepted the unique handmade piece of jewelry knowing that it belonged to a town member who lived during the latter half of the nineteenth century and was most likely made there as well.

Letters and Personal Correspondence—Always

All personal letters have historical significance. Consider the privacy and confidentiality of the people who wrote the letters, received the letters, or get mentioned in the letters, and protect it when advisable—it's one of those areas in which the Golden Rule provides a good guide—but keep them, especially if they reveal distress and dysfunction. The dark side of life explains decisions and behaviors that records usually leave out but that historians need for a complete picture of what life contained. You can protect privacy by putting the letters into a folder and putting them out of reach of others. If you donate them to a repository, ask that it close them until their contents will not harm anybody. (See "Privacy" in chapter 7.)

Donald, his family's "historian," had pulled together a family genealogy, photographs, documents, letters, and correspondence pertaining to the lives of his parents, Edmund and Miriam. Edmund had served in the army during World War II and the couple's war correspondence was particularly rich, offering their opinions on the social responsibilities of married couples, politics, the progression of the war, and their heartfelt love for one another. Edmund wrote a lengthy letter immediately after D-Day in which he describes in detail the events and his reactions of that battle. Later, Edmund graphically describes some of the sights he witnesses; especially chilling were his references to the concentration camps and "labor reform" prisons. Miriam never wanted the letters to be seen by her children or anyone else because they contained such tragic wartime descriptions and sensual professions of love between husband and wife that she felt no one should read. After his parents' death, Donald approached the local historical society about accepting the family papers. He realized the value contained in the letters alone. The historical society was delighted to have the family papers to add to their World War II Veterans collection.

Libraries—Rarely

You may find a library of books that someone put together as part of his or her professional activities over a lifetime of working. Similarly, you may find a collection of books kept together over several generations. Both of these types of libraries might interest a collecting institution, because they show what a particular person or a family read at a particular time. But they will take up a lot of space.

Professional libraries can provide a rich glimpse into the changing of a profession or the breadth of interest of a member of a particular profession. Such libraries may interest the individual's alma mater or the archives of a professional organization, but most will not interest a local historical society. CAPCAS applies.

Almost no repository will want the general collection of books that accumulated over the course of a sixty-year marriage spent in one house.

David, a retired music professor and author of several academic books, did a great deal of research before deciding where to donate his professional library of reference, research, and rare books pertaining to early American music. He could have donated his library to his alma mater, a large university that already had many of the more recent publications David had collected. Instead, he decided to donate his collection to a music library and archive specializing in his subject area. This way, David's collection would stay intact and be available to scholars in that particular field of study. He and the library came to an agreement whereby any duplicate or otherwise inappropriate books found in the donation could be sold by the archive with the proceeds going to the cataloging and care of the rare book collection.

Manuscripts and Professional Papers—Always

Over a lifetime of working, a person might accumulate a vast quantity of papers, including correspondence, clippings, and writings related to managing a business or professional practice. Within the context of that person's life, all the papers have historical value. Beyond what they say about the individual, they show us how previous generations responded to the recurring issues of life and work—regardless of what work they did. A farmer's records have as much value as a lawyer's or politician's to a researcher looking for primary information on the subject. Records and papers kept by women, children, and members of minorities are relatively rare, therefore, have even more value.

Medical Records—Maybe

Medical records can have high historical worth, but they also carry a lot of privacy issues and may be subject to certain privacy laws. Like letters and diaries, you may want to keep them private until after any information they contain will not hurt anyone. After that, they can offer valuable insight into many aspects of health and health care issues. (See "Privacy" in chapter 7.)

Neil, a very bright, hardworking farm boy born in 1932 in southeast Ohio, expected to continue his family's long tradition of farming. However, he excelled in the local schools and, in the 1950s, received an academic scholarship to Harvard, where he got his BA. He then went on to the PhD program at the University of Wisconsin, and his proud parents did everything they could to support him. Toward the end of the PhD program, all doctoral students had to take a series of general exams to determine whether they should go on to the dissertation phase. While Neil studied for those exams, he idly wondered why his mother's letters were postmarked "Parkersburg, WV." Years later, after the death of both his parents, an uncle explained that his father had suffered a stroke and was in a hospital in Parkersburg. His parents didn't want to upset him during a stressful time, and didn't tell him. Nor did they ever tell him. When he learned about the stroke, he was grateful that they had spared him at the time, but he wished he had some form of record to get a sense of what had really happened.

Musical Instruments—Maybe

Music has always played an important role in human society, so it makes sense that most historical repositories have some musical materials in their collections. Those areas with rich musical traditions including community orchestras, town bands, school bands, music festivals, professional musicians, household musicians, religious groups, military bands, and the music industry will have more. Handmade musical instruments belonging to any of these groups may have historical significance, especially if they belonged to someone notable or are unique and obsolete. Certainly a museum will seek instruments from geographic and cultural regions where they are traditionally played and have the most relevance. CAPCAS applies.

Photographs—Always

"A picture is worth a thousand words" rings true when we hold an image of a subject from long ago and it conveys a lot of information without words. Most families have photographs of people, places, buildings, events, animals, and things that capture a moment in time and tell stories. These have historical significance if they portray identifiable people, places, buildings, and events that no longer exist, and if the information accompanies them. Any older images without any identifying information, for example, a group of unnamed young people posing on an unnamed beach, have little historical value, but a picture of the same

A collection of family photographs.
Credit: LiliGraphie.

group of unnamed young people posing in a park across from an identifiable block of buildings carries information about the changes made to the buildings in the background. The most useful images carry the following information: the identity of any living creatures in the shot; the date, place, event; the name of the photographer, and the photographer's interest in the picture he or she took.

A retired reporter bought a small community newspaper and the building it occupied. After a year of ownership, he decided he had no use for the forty-year archive of photos that the previous two owners had accumulated. He offered them to the local historical society, which instantly accepted them and the four five-drawer filing cabinets they occupied. It took three years for the volunteers to compare the images against the published versions and copy the identifying information from the newspaper captions to the backs of the photos themselves. The historical society then filed them in a way to make them easily accessible and found that it used this rich collection of local images almost daily.

Digital cameras make taking pictures easy and cheap—no film to buy and no developing to pay for. You probably don't need all the images you took at your child's first birthday party, but you do want to keep some to pass down to later generations and perhaps a historical repository. We discuss the preservation of digital documents in chapter 8, and will merely say here that, for the sake of history, you should print out the pictures you want to keep over time. Chapter 8 also has much more information about preserving photographs.

Mr. Young opened a photographic studio in a small Western town during the 1940s. Always interested in history, he collected old albumen prints, cartes de visite, tintypes, daguerreotypes, photographs, and other images of people and places in the area throughout his lifetime. At one point, he found, in a barn, boxes of glass plates from a previous photography studio that operated after the Civil War. All together, Mr. Young accumulated tens of thousands of images and negatives that recorded the history of the county from roughly 1860 to 1980. Mr. Young's son, Doug, inherited the family business as well as the valuable historical image collection. Doug wasn't interested in history; he wanted to make money, and he decided to keep the collection and charge a fee to anyone who wanted to see or use the images. Immediately problems appeared. The images had no order to them, so users had trouble finding what they wanted. Doug didn't have enough money to preserve the wide variety of types of historic images, and allowing people to hunt through them indiscriminately immediately caused damage.

Doug received pressure from the community to make the images freely available. After several years, Doug realized how highly the community valued the photographs, so he donated his dad's historic photography collection to the county archives. He retained copyright of all of the images his father had created, and occasionally received a royalty payment for images people published, but the tax deduction for the value of the gift and the goodwill from the community more than made up for the money he originally thought he could make from the individual sale of copies.

Quilts

(See "Household Linens")

Recipe Cards and Cookbooks — Usually

Boxes of handwritten recipes reflect what people ate and how they cured common ailments. If the cards in the box indicate the source of the recipe, they also document the communication patterns among women. Recipe cards and cookbooks straddle the line between handwritten and mass-produced instructions for cooking. Typically recipe cards contain handwritten recipes—many of them from other people's cookbooks. They may also contain recipes cut from magazines. Cookbooks come with their own set of recipes, but cooks regularly annotate them with reviews or changes of ingredients. Regardless, they are important in that they reflect the eating tastes and habits of their time and place.

Women who migrate from one country to another often carry their recipes with them so they can maintain a sense of home, even in a strange land. In many cases, however, they must experiment with local ingredients to get the flavors they want, because staples in their place of origin do not exist in their new home. How they make this transition will likely appear in the cookbook in some way, and it will add rich details to many historians' work.

Cookbooks from local clubs and groups also reflect the cooking styles of particular areas, groups, or times. Such cookbooks are often compiled as a fund-raising activity for groups like women's clubs or the women's auxiliary of a church or fraternal organization. These cookbooks not only provide information about cooking, but also about members of the publishing group. Sometimes they include brief histories about the town or group, the contributors, or their families. Many companies also produced cookbooks to teach homemakers how to use new products or devices. These cookbooks often have illustrations that provide a wealth of information about changes in food production methods, as well as advertising, design, and fashion. All of these materials can prove to be valuable to museums or archives. CAPCAS applies.

Recorded Sound — Maybe

Through the years, we have listened to music on a variety of media and changing technologies on which to play them, including Edison cylinders, wire recordings, 78 rpm, 45 rpm, 33⅓ rpm discs, vinyl LPs, reel-to-reel tapes, cassette tapes, 8-track tapes, compact discs, and now digital files. Unusual recording formats sometimes appear as well—picture discs, discs of 3"–5" or 16"–20", recordings found on the backs of cereal boxes, and the like. Most households contain some type of sound recordings and their historical significance depends upon the format, the condition, the content, and their context. Unique recordings of local events, concerts,

Obsolete recorded sound formats, such as cylinder wire, tape, and transcription disc that require obsolete and hard-to-find playback equipment.
From the Collections of the Center for Popular Music, Middle Tennessee State University, Murfreesboro.

festivals, or nonmusical events such as speeches and interviews will interest local repositories. However, the ability to play the media may present problems. Conserving, preserving, and transferring unique recordings of older formats warrant the money and effort it will cost, depending on the recording's condition and rarity. Most historical repositories will not want commercial sound recordings, but some might. Those specialized repositories that do will only need examples, however, but it may be worth contacting one of these if you have significant collections. CAPCAS applies.

Mildred contacted an archive specializing in music and recorded sound because she had a collection of her father's work that she wanted to place where it would be cared for and used by students and researchers. Her father had been a music publisher and singer in a men's quartet during the 1930s–1940s. One of the items in the collection was a large 16" recording disc with four holes in the center label instead of just one. The label had nothing on it but straight lines. The record, too big to play on a regular turntable, did not look like a commercial recording. The audio specialist at the music archive recognized the 16" recording as an electrical transcription or transcription disc made exclusively for radio broadcasting during the "Golden Age of Radio."

The music archive maintained an audio preservation laboratory where they could transfer most forms of recorded media to digital formats. The technician played the recording for Mildred, and, to everyone's surprise, it turned out to be a recording of her father singing in his quartet and then talking about his music and the quartet with someone in the radio station. What made this particularly poignant was the fact that Mildred's father had died before she and her twin brother had turned two, and neither could recall hearing his voice. The archive gave Mildred a digital recording of the transcription disc, and she said it was the best gift she had ever received.

Religious Materials — Maybe

Handmade objects and documents related to the practice and practitioners of a particular religion may interest a repository, especially if the materials relate to religious groups founded locally. A wide variety of religious books and artifacts can create a picture of religious groups and their roles in local histories. (See "Religious Materials" in chapter 3.)

School Materials — Maybe

Many of us have school papers, reports, tests, notebooks, etc. These probably have more sentimental value than historical. However, some school materials have historical significance and end up in history museums or archives. Around the nation you can find examples of nineteenth- and early twentieth-century school rooms re-created. Many museums themselves are housed in former school buildings. Copy books from the nineteenth century that show lessons in reading, good penmanship, and arithmetic are historically significant, as would be most school papers from the nineteenth century due to their scarcity. In the early nineteen century, students most likely had a slate board and chalk. A museum would welcome the slate board. As the century progressed, paper, scissors, glue, pencils, and books became available for each child. Therefore, mid- to late twentieth-century student creations are more abundant and may be historically noteworthy, depending on whether they are from a local family or notable person or serve to fulfill some purpose needed by a local repository. Educational lesson plans and teacher resources and aids may also have relevance. Methods and materials used in teaching change with society, so the materials created by students of this generation will also be historically significant. CAPCAS applies

Scrapbooks — Usually

Scrapbooks document the creator's perspective on some interest: their personal life, one or more organizations, and/or events. Fascinating as they are, scrapbooks reflect the person who put them together, and the significance of elements may escape everyone else. Scrapbooks also show current traditions and graphic styles. If a scrapbook has no meaning to you, include it with the maker's papers in a donation to an archive, where researchers might look for meaning in the collected materials.

> When Peggy's mother passed away, she had no idea what she was going to do with the many scrapbooks her mother had in her house. Her friends called her "Scrapbook Queen." She made scrapbooks for herself and her friends as a hobby. Peggy gave the friends their scrapbooks—easy decision. A few of the others she kept for herself because they documented her own family. Some scrapbooks covered local events, and those she offered to the local historical society. Peggy also found scrapbooks that had belonged to her grandmother. One contained nothing but newspaper and magazine clippings of service men and women from the Alabama county her grandmother lived in during World War II. Using the internet, Peggy found the local historical society and offered the World War II scrapbook to them. They were delighted to have such a compilation of materials. Along with it, Peggy sent a biography of her grandmother and mother, who grew up in the town, and a monetary gift for the care of the scrapbook.

Taxidermy — Rarely

Mounted hunting trophies have little historical significance. Further, they can be difficult to care for, and can be very hard to store, which means that they present more challenges than benefits for a local historical society. If you have a mounted trophy killed by a very famous person or the mounted remains of a very famous animal, maybe a repository that collects taxidermy would want it. Probably not a local historical society.

Tools—Usually

Handmade tools have historical value, and some have an added quality as works of art. Historical repositories might want obsolete or unique tools that have a local connection or signify some element the museum wants to interpret in their exhibits. Museums may also wish to include handmade tools in their educational programs or for props. If you are not sure about a tool's identification, consult an expert before disposing of it. CAPCAS applies.

Handmade tools in a wooden box.

Toys—Usually

A handmade toy will most likely be historically valuable if it was made before the era of mass production. Museums hold many handmade wooden toys of the eighteenth and nineteenth centuries, as well as those made of cloth, leather, iron, and other organic materials. Handmade toys, like their manufactured counterparts, reflect the social and cultural values, events, and available materials of a certain time and place. Handmade toys also reveal the skill and methods of their maker. A hometown repository may be eager to acquire a toy that was made by someone locally or belonging to a notable person. Hand manufacture, ownership, and uniqueness makes such items, even in fairly new toys, historically valuable to repositories. CAPCAS applies.

Wills, Probate, and Related Documents—Always

They all have historical value. Wills and probate documents can give a genealogist or a historian valuable information about a family, their relations and neighbors, local customs for caring for the dead, as well as the financial well-being of the person who died. Probate documents usually describe a person's property and its disposition after death, as well as give indications as to whether someone could read or write, how much estate tax they paid, and other financial and material details associated with someone's death and the settlement of their estate. Not everyone has a will, but there may be other documents that settled an estate or made arrangements for old age care before they died.

NOTE

1. See Center for Home Movies, accessed December 31, 2017, http://centerfor homemovies.org/yours.

5

Historical Value:
Corporate Material

We use the term *corporate* here in a very broadly defined way—any entity that has a governing body to oversee its work. We include for-profit business and not-for-profit or ganizations of all kinds. As a sector, corporations create an enormous amount of documents and artifacts. Some have historical value, and while archives will probably accept most of what you have to offer, after museums have examples of what they want, they might accept a replacement in better condition, but they won't want to add more to their collection just for the sake of having more. If you offer a repository something, the acquisitions people will look closely for the right mixture of condition, age, provenance, completeness, and available space at their repository—we've abbreviated the concept of those collective qualities as CAPCAS.

Condition refers to how little damage an item has suffered; the less damage, the better. Age generally means the older the better, but it can mean something from a specific time. Provenance refers to the history of who owned or used the item over its lifetime. Items owned and/or used by important people have more historical value than those owned or used by nobody in particular. Completeness refers to whether all the parts and pieces remain with the item—a hotel register with all its pages or a tool with all its moving parts. Finally, the repository will assess whether it has Available Space to store responsibly the item you're offering. An archive or museum will apply CAPCAS criteria to business materials as readily as it will to personal goods.

EVALUATION OF CORPORATE RECORDS

Here, we list a range of corporate records and give a one-word evaluation for the historical value of them. We use the scale "Always, Usually, Maybe, Rarely, Never" to evaluate historical significance; the description also adds more detail. We add the phrase "CAPCAS applies" to indicate

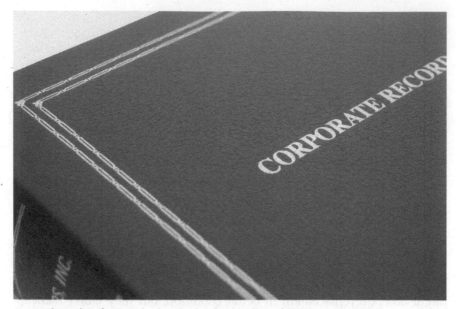

One volume in what can be hundreds of cubic feet of corporate records.

how a repository will assess something from this category if you offer it to their collection.

Business Records—Maybe

Business records can have enormous historical value. They explain the numbers that drive the economic history of the company or organization they track, and that organization or company may have had an enormous impact on an entire region. But business records come as huge collections of governance records, correspondence, marketing ideas, promotional materials, personnel records, and financial documents—a complete universe. They require a lot of storage space and require a lot of time to use because of their volume. If you find that you have business records for a defunct business, you might want to place them in an archives, but don't take offense if the repository declines them. Because they take up so much space, and because using them takes highly specialized knowledge and skill, very few researchers will attempt to use them. Take heart in the knowledge that larger repositories might accept what smaller ones will not. Active businesses may have their own archives that would welcome early records.

A large stack of unprocessed business papers.

On a Thursday afternoon, the new owner of the local newspaper invited Harriet, a professional archivist and the president of the local historical society, to take anything she wanted from the upper two floors of the newspaper building he had just bought along with the business. He suggested that she start with the second floor, because he had scheduled the local garbage hauler to come and clear out all the paper Saturday morning. Harriet accepted his invitation and did an immediate quick survey of what she had said yes to. To her astonishment, she found two rooms filled to the brim with business records, reporters' notebooks, subject files, published reports, computer manuals, competitor newspapers, government documents, and books. The other three rooms held similar materials.

When she returned the following morning, she had made a few decisions. (1) She would take only a sample of the business records from the years the records represented. While she knew the business records held a lot of historical value, none of the researchers who came to her archives would have any interest in them; the business records would merely take up space other materials could occupy. (2) She would take only a sample of the reporters' notebooks to show how reporters had used them. Most had no name on them, and none had a date. All portrayed the idiosyncratic style of the person taking the notes, and Harriet realized that a researcher would have to work extremely hard to make any sense of them. As a small local historical society, her collection didn't attract that kind of researcher, and the notebooks would take up a lot of space. (3) She would take none of the competing newspapers; researchers could find them other places.

She then spent six hours going through the rest of the papers. She repeatedly asked herself (1) where else a researcher might find a book, a published report, or a government document; (2) what she could take samples of; and (3) what her researchers valued most. At the end of the day, she walked away with about ten boxes of "good stuff." The third floor, which she did in a much more leisurely way, yielded a similar amount of material based on the same rules.

Business Machines — Rarely

Business machines of all types can have historical significance as evidence of how business processes have changed. However, for a repository, the value of any business machine will come from (1) the type of machine or (2) who used it. A typewriter used by a prominent writer might interest a repository that houses the writer's papers. CAPCAS strongly applies.

Club and Organizational Records — Usually

The records of clubs and social or professional organizations contain a wealth of information about their activities and about the members and community. Local archives or the main archives of a national organization may find them historically valuable. Records from these clubs might provide a record of club activities as well as a history of the changing role of the people in the club, and a history of the life of individuals in their communities. Many local historical societies would welcome these.

Financial Records — Maybe

Old financial records can have great historical significance. While more difficult to interpret than letters and diaries, financial data have more credibility than anecdotal data. In many cases, the financial data explain the reality behind stories that appear in diaries and letters.

Privacy laws now cover current financial records, especially if they include credit card numbers or social security numbers. Financial advisors caution that things like tax records and bank account records should be kept for a certain amount of time and then shredded. In this age of identity theft, we understand the reason, but we lament the loss of these valuable historical records.

Instructional Manuals—Maybe

Instructional manuals, such as those giving the operational particulars for a machine or those explaining a special skill such as sign language for the deaf, generally fall under the category of ephemera. As such, they

Instructional manuals from different types of machines and appliances over several decades.

have some historical value and might interest an archives or museum, especially if the repository has a device to go with the book. They may have additional significance depending upon who owned them, when they were written, why they were kept, or if they accompany the machine they describe.

Licenses — Rarely

A license acknowledges that the holder has successfully proved a certain competence at a particular task or that the holder has passed a test and paid a fee to operate a certain tool or perform a specified activity. Most licenses, such as a person's driver's license, a hunting license, or a software license, do not have historic significance except as part of the personal papers of the owner; nor do professional licenses you see hanging on walls in a place of business. (See "Diplomas" in chapter 6.)

Occupational Equipment and Goods — Usually

Most occupations have associated equipment. Farmers, blacksmiths, tailors, druggists, teachers, doctors, jewelers, bankers, and so on, all have special tools. A local museum might want any equipment or tools belong-

Large metal ice tongs are an example of a now obsolete occupational tool.

ing to a local community trade or business, especially if that trade or business no longer exists. The historical significance of the items lies in their significance to economic expansion and changes over time.

> Lucy inherited metal ice tongs that her grandfather used to carry large blocks of ice from the icehouse to the truck that distributed the ice to people's houses in central Alabama during the 1930s and 1940s. At each home, he used the ice tongs again to put the blocks into customers' iceboxes—large wooden pieces of furniture lined with metal to keep the ice from melting. Now an obsolete occupational tool that a museum might want, ice tongs cast light on how people kept things cold before the invention of refrigerators.

Photographs—Always

Images of corporate operations, especially those taken by the corporate body, show an aspect of most corporate entities that don't commonly appear in personal or family papers. They have strong historical value if you can identify the subject or place they depict. Visual images need textual descriptions to explain them. Document as much about visual images as you can, as soon as you can. Identify any people, processes, and locations in photographs, and explain why the corporate body took the picture. Was it applying for disaster relief after a tragedy, or was this a shot intended for a fund-raising campaign? You can see how the use of the picture might affect how they staged the image. Even if you can't identify an image, someone else might; ask around. If you can identify the image, write the information on the back using a soft pencil. If the "paper" the photo was printed on has more plastic than paper in it, put the information on a piece of paper and put it and the photo in an envelope.

Political Ephemera—Always

All types of objects and paper from political events in the broadest sense interest local history organizations: placards and yard signs for local candidates, manuscripts with speeches and political strategies, political premiums like coffee mugs or dishes, as well as buttons and medals for various races and causes. These highly significant political ephemera of all types—local, state, and national—often are thrown out after the election or campaign. Rather than throwing it all away, consider offering it to an archive or a museum.

A collection of political buttons.

Premiums and Prizes—Maybe

Premiums and prizes come in two forms: purchase premiums and prize premiums.

Purchase premiums, the trading card variety, created an incentive for someone to purchase a product. Another type required the consumer to redeem one or more proof-of-purchase coupons for a prize, which usually had the company's logo emblazoned on it. Premiums obtained by redeeming savings stamps are another example of this type of prize. As a genre, such prizes are like ephemera. A local or regional museum or archives might find such objects of interest, particularly if they reflect a certain time or a local company.

Prize premiums come in the form of substantial rewards of money and some sort of ribbon, plaque, trophy, or medal recognizing an improvement in a process or product. The most common that may appear in your attic are prizes and ribbons awarded at county and state fairs. Depending on their rarity, awards of this type may have historical interest. CAPCAS applies.

Religious Materials—Usually

Corporate religious materials have historical value because they illuminate the practices and heritage of local faiths. All manner of religious organizations, societies, and orders have a corporate archive dedicated to the preservation and access of their business papers, objects, and documents. Local membership records, business meeting minutes, financial records, cemetery records, legal documents, insurance policies, architectural drawings, annual reports, photographs, and objects unique to that particular organization serve to create a vital portrait of a religious community and its members. If you have a collection of such materials, keep them, or contact a local repository, but be aware that a regional, state, or national religious archive might also want your collection to fill in holes in its own.

A community of Laotian refugees resettled in a small town in North Carolina in the 1970s and founded a church they called the First Church. The church's revivals, special events, Laotian holidays, educational programs, and guest speakers from Laos and Thailand provided a conduit between the Laotian and American cultures. The Keophothong family was especially active in the church's creation and activities through the decades. After the family elders died, the family prepared to sell their house and found a box of materials labeled "Church" in Laotian. It contained incorporation documents for the First Church, along with photographs, programs, and various other business and financial records. Membership records showed that membership had dropped from 125 to 30 members by the year 2000, the year the church merged with another congregation in the area. The merged church's governing body sold the First Church's property to a developer who demolished the building in early 2002. Copies of newspaper articles about the sale and demolition included with the papers, along with correspondence, pamphlets, and materials connected with the church's activities told a rich and remarkably complete story of the church's existence. The Keophothong family donated the box of papers to the local historical society, which was delighted to accept—especially because of the First Church's excellent example of working to mobilize a community to reach out to other cultures and to build positive understandings.

6

Historical Value: Commemorative Material

It's hard to throw away something that documents an accomplishment. As a result, most people have diplomas, medals, ribbons, plaques, trophies, and other assorted inscribed items that symbolize a hard-won victory. They have huge personal and sentimental value, but do they have historical value?

While archives will probably accept most of what you have to offer, museums have to select more carefully. After they have examples of what they want, they might accept a replacement in better condition, but they won't want to add more of anything to their collection just for the sake of having more. If you offer a repository something, the acquisitions people will look closely for the right mixture of condition, age, provenance, completeness, and available space at their repository—we've abbreviated the concept of those collective qualities as CAPCAS.

Condition refers to how little damage an item has suffered; the less damage, the better. Age generally means the older the better, but it can mean something from a specific time. Provenance refers to the history of who owned or used the item over its lifetime. Items owned and/or used by important people have more historical value than those owned or used by nobody in particular. Completeness refers to whether all the parts and pieces remain with the item—a hotel register with all its pages or a tool with all its moving parts. Finally, the repository will assess whether it has Available Space to store responsibly the item you're offering. A museum will apply CAPCAS criteria to commemorative materials as readily as it will to other materials.

EVALUATION OF COMMEMORATIVE MATERIAL

Here, we list a range of commemorative materials and give a one-word evaluation for the historical value of them. We use the scale "Always, Usually, Maybe, Rarely, Never" to evaluate historical significance; the description also adds more detail. We add the phrase "CAPCAS applies" to indicate how a repository will assess something from this category if you offer it to their collection.

Awards and Certificates — Rarely

Awards and certificates, either documents or objects, commemorate a person's noteworthy accomplishments but convey no legal right to do anything. Like diplomas and licenses, these have historical significance as part of an individual's collection of papers, but as a single document or object, they have almost no historical value. Though an engraved silver tray, crystal bowl, or a precious metal medal has some monetary value, the personalization may diminish it. Plaques and framed paper awards without the context of the life of the person referenced on the form have little historical value. The granting body keeps records of people to whom it issues awards, certificates, or diplomas, and a historian will turn there if he or she wants to find names of recipients. (*See also* "Diplomas" and "Trophies.")

Graduation gowns are a form of ceremonial clothing.

Mary's late husband had gained international prominence in his career, and she donated his files to the Special Collections Department of the university where he had taught. She knew that the dozen or so plaques he had received for various awards would take up a lot of space for very little information, but she didn't want the awards to go undocumented. She photocopied each of the plaques and included the photocopies with his papers. She kept the plaques for herself.

Clothing—Maybe

All clothing, especially ceremonial garb, carries stories, and, depending on the story, may have historical significance. It can serve to interpret American work, play, religion, fashion, culture, economic class, politics, and more. Ceremonial clothing may include wedding dresses, religious garments, uniforms, costumes, and apparel worn at graduations, parades, and school proms. Even T-shirts with slogans from a political campaign or a favorite band concert fall into this category. Clothing made by

Oaklands Mansion in Murfreesboro, Tennessee brings one hundred years of fashion, culture, and community history to life through locally loaned and donated wedding dresses and their stories in the "Wedding Dresses Through the Decades" exhibit.
Ken Robinson Photography.

a well-known brand or fashion designer during the mass-manufacturing era may have historical value. The same applies to earlier handmade or tailored apparel. Ceremonial clothing from a previous era; of a particular fabric or mode of construction; or by a particular dressmaker, tailor, or fashion house might raise interest as "vintage" or as examples. Clothing value depends very much upon condition and completeness. The same assessment applies to accessories, such as hats, collars, handbags, and so on. CAPCAS applies.

WEDDING DRESSES

Wedding dresses carry loads of sentiment within a family, making them hard to discard. While important to families, they probably have little historical value, depending on the circumstances surrounding the gown, such as who wore it, when and where, the gown's maker, its story, and its condition. Because of their size and the complexity of their construction, they require a lot of care and usually require large storage boxes and areas in which to store them, so adequate space and funds must also be available to the museum. House museums have created popular exhibits of local wedding dresses for which community members loan wedding gowns, photographs, and other items and share their stories and memories of their weddings. Some of the gowns end up in the community museum representing wedding styles and local history through the ages, but CAPCAS plays a very large role in the decision-making process.

ACCESSORIES

Hats, handbags, purses, belts, gloves, stockings, collars, shoes, scarves, and other accessories to clothing may be important historically if they commemorate an important event in the life of an individual or the community. Condition will matter to a repository, especially in the case of shoes and hats, which tend to be made of organic materials and receive a great deal of wear. Older hats with feathers may also fall under the Migratory Bird Treaty Act of 1918. (*See* "Wildlife Protection" in chapter 7.)

DOCUMENTATION

If you find receipts, boxes, bags, tags, directions, advertisements, patterns, or other documents that obviously belong with commemorative clothing items, save them—they can increase the historical value of the piece and add a great deal of information. For instance, if you find academic regalia with its original invoice, you have a much richer and understandable object. Photographs of people wearing the clothing or item would also obviously add to the historical significance.

Diplomas — Rarely

Education institutions grant diplomas to certify that the recipient has completed a particular course or received a particular degree. You often see physicians and lawyers post their diplomas on the walls of their offices as a demonstration that they have attained the education required to practice their profession. Diplomas have historic significance to the person who earned them and should stay with the person's professional or personal papers. Schools keep records of their graduates, but a diploma is a personal and public memento of a significant achievement. (*See also* "Licenses" in chapter 5.)

High school and college diplomas from family members.

Trophies — Rarely

Mass-produced trophies that every member of a winning team received probably have more value to your family than to a local museum. However, very old trophies of interesting design and singular or unusual trophies have historical significance and will interest most repositories.

An older trophy.

Note that many older trophies were made of precious metals like silver or gold plate. If you decide to dispose of a trophy, make sure you don't throw away metal you could reclaim or sell as scrap. The same holds true for individual medals awarded for participation in sports competitions. (*See* "Awards and Certificates" and "Diplomas.")

The High Plains Historical Society (HPHS) accepted all the trophies the principal found in the Prairieville Elementary School building. Thirty years earlier, the community's school system, Prairieville Schools (PS), which had educated local children since the late 1800s, had joined a union district for educating its high school students and tore down the old PS building to make way for the new Prairieville Elementary School building. Many in the community who had attended PS remembered it fondly, and when the crews cleaned out the old PS building, they couldn't bring themselves to throw away the collection of trophies the school had acquired over its history. Instead, a crew packed them up and put them with the materials to go into the new elementary school when it opened. After thirty years, the Prairieville Elementary School administration no longer felt any emotional connection to its collection of more than sixty trophies that dated back into the 1920s, and it needed room for its own trophies. It offered the PS trophies to the HPHS.

The volunteers at the HPHS, most of them PS graduates, remembered many of the events that the trophies represented and accepted them all without question. For the next fifteen years, the boxes of trophies were sorted and resorted, packed and repacked, and moved and moved again within the HPHS's limited storage area. They took up a lot of space. Eventually an HPHS committee made up of people who had not graduated from PS, sorted the collection by event type, year, award, and trophy type, thereby whittling the collection to about half the original number. They sold a few of the culls—mostly to members of the team that had won them—discarded the broken ones, and put the rest away to go into their next garage sale. Such was the symbolic power of the trophies, that even a dispassionate committee could not risk the community ire by just discarding them.

7

Special Issues

Most of the materials you will encounter do not provide any problem at all, but issues may crop up that you should recognize. We include this chapter to raise your awareness of those issues so you can decide whether you want to ask for professional advice.

OWNERSHIP

While you may think about the contents of your attic as belonging to "the family," the law requires precision. The law gives the owner the right to make the final decision about something's care and disposition, so before you make decisions, you should know who—legally—owns what. The owner may not have *custody* of his or her possessions, but he or she still has the last say about them.

A deceased person's will or trust documents usually designates the next owner of financially valuable property, but, the documents may say nothing about items with little beyond sentimental or historical value. That omission can lead to problems over who decides their fate. If family members see ownership of family materials as some loose form of group ownership, making decisions can suffer from a lack of a formal framework or articulated rules, regulations, and processes. Conflicts can erupt. To avoid family conflict and to preserve a family's historical legacy as a whole piece, the family must work out ways to resolve ownership issues.

Typically, ownership of a deceased person's goods passes to the primary beneficiary. If no will exists, individual state laws provide guidance as to who should control distribution of an estate, and often that person has the power to determine the disposition of family papers and artifacts. Some families designate a person to care for the family's historical legacy. That person should act in a clear and forthright manner, keeping all family members apprised of discussions, suggestions, and decisions concerning the disposition of the materials. He or she should handle any conflicts before they become problems, and negotiate a solution that will balance family wishes with the longevity of the family's historical legacy. If legal questions arise, the designated person should seek professional help.

COPYRIGHTS AND PATENTS

In Article I, Section 8, Clause 8 of the American Constitution, the founders laid the groundwork for our current laws by giving Congress the power "To promote the progress of science and useful arts, by securing for limited times to authors and inventors the exclusive right to their respective writings and discoveries." The framers saw these rights as economic fairness—a writer should be paid for his or her work, and an inventor should also—but for a limited amount of time, lest they stifle creativity and competition.

Copyright laws can get very complicated, but the basic idea amounts to this: The creator of a written composition, painting, photographic image, or digital work should get acknowledgment for and a portion of the profits derived from that work. So, if you find an essay that an ancestor wrote fifty years ago, you violate copyright laws if you get paid for publishing it under your own name. Patent laws provide the same protection for inventions.

Note that patent and copyright laws do not protect an idea; they protect the expression of an idea. Where would the music industry be if one person had a copyright on saying "I love you" with music? Every writer of a love song writes on the same theme, but each owns the copyright to his or her particular way of expressing it. The same holds for the designers of jewelry or tools. Anybody can claim ownership of a design for something decorative to wear on one's finger or to pound something into place, so long as nobody else has created exactly the same design for a ring or a hammer.

NATIVE AMERICAN ANTIQUITIES, ARTS, AND CRAFTS

In the latter half of the nineteenth century, publicity about railroad access to American Indian arts and crafts raised the public's desire to own them. The demand encouraged the revival of certain craft traditions, and tribes started to produce items specifically designed for the tourist trade. Outside the marketplace, people also just grabbed them when they found them.

Since 1906, federal laws have protected the dwelling sites and artifacts left behind on federal land by the people who lived there before the European conquest and settlement. Federal law also protects sites sacred to the religions of Native Americans.

If you find American Indian artifacts in your family attic, understand that disposing of them has become complicated—both legally and ethically. Unless you come from an American Indian family, you need to find out, preferably through documentation, whether they came from private property, public land, Indian mounds, or burial sites. Thoroughly investigate the provenance of what you find.

No regular "Native American Antiquities Police Force" exists, so you will not likely get into legal trouble if you find something the law does not allow you to own; you just cannot do much with it. As soon as you try to sell it, you may attract legal attention to yourself. You can offer such items to a museum, but museums may balk at taking them. If you don't want them, consider returning them to the tribe that created them.

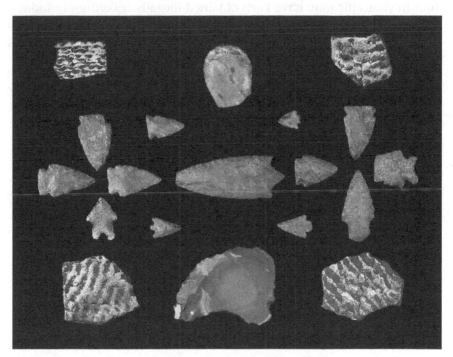

A collection of Native American arrowheads and pottery shards.

ARCHAEOLOGICAL OR ANTHROPOLOGICAL SPECIMENS

Artifacts and materials found buried underground belong to the category called archaeological and anthropological specimens. These include Native American arrowheads, spear points, beads, stone tools, bones, and the relics unearthed through metal detectors. Archaeology and anthropology as scientific disciplines encompass the study of humankind from its origins to the present day. They have perfected excavation, recording, and archiving techniques proven to protect valuable historical content and information. When an amateur collector digs into an archaeological site, the digging destroys the physical material and valuable contextual information that may have been gleaned from the study of the site. Thus, because archaeological sites and historical places are fragile, irreplaceable, and nonrenewable historical resources, various state and federal laws protect them and the materials removed from them. Today, it is illegal to collect artifacts from federal lands, such as National Parks, National Forests, or military bases. Some states also have laws against the removal of prehistoric artifacts. Therefore, the ancient artifacts you might find in your attic may have been obtained illegally according to today's laws, which makes knowing where your collection of artifacts came from important. Even if you do not know the provenance, consider contacting a museum about your collection of archaeological or anthropological materials. If a museum accepts your collection, your donation will contribute to our scientific understanding of the past, rather than hiding in obscurity or being destroyed.

WILDLIFE PROTECTION

To protect wildlife—mostly migratory birds killed to adorn ladies' fashions—from extinction, the federal government passed a number of laws that make it illegal to own feathers or parts of protected birds without a permit or proof that your family acquired the bird parts before the passage of the laws.

Many states have their own antiquities and wildlife protection laws that might apply. As with antiquities, if you find something that belongs in this category, you cannot do much with it without attracting legal attention, and a museum will probably balk if you offer it to them.

A ladies' hat adorned with a stuffed bird.

PRIVACY

The privacy of individuals whose things wind up in the attic can present both legal and ethical issues.

Because database technology, combined with the Internet, has made searching and sorting personal information so easy, laws now protect certain aspects of a person's private information: (1) social security numbers and other unique numbers that might lead to identity theft, and (2) current financial records, including credit card numbers, credit reports, tax records, and medical records. Governments and financial institutions have guidelines for the length of time you should keep such records for non-historical purposes.[1] If your attic contains these types of records, which can have great historic importance, and if you decide to deposit those family records in a public archives, don't worry. Professionally trained archivists are highly sensitive to and have great concern for issues of privacy and confidentiality. They will protect people's private information in accordance with the law and the policies in their institutions. Those policies frequently go beyond the demands of the law. If you have any concerns, you could redact Social Security numbers and various account numbers before you turn them over.

The privacy rules in the Health Insurance Portability and Accountability Act of 1996 (HIPAA) protect an individual's medical records for fifty years after the individual's death. During those fifty years, the personal representative with authority to act on behalf of the decedent may allow selected people to use the records. That does not mean that you must protect those records for fifty years. If you have the authority of the personal representative, you may destroy them or place them in a repository if it will accept them.

REPLEVIN

Replevin is a legal action in which Person A claims that Person B unjustly holds something that belongs to Person A, and she or he wants it back. This can suddenly become an issue as you sort through the collections in the attic. Perhaps Person A loaned it to Person B for a set period of time, and that time has gone by. Perhaps Person A lost it, and Person B found it and will not return it. Perhaps someone stole it from Person A and gave it or sold it to Person B. Replevin does not imply guilt for any wrongdoing beyond holding property that the plaintiff wants back. A replevin action seeks to recover the actual property, not its monetary value.

A replevin action can arise between any two parties that can sue or be sued in court—people, corporate bodies, and governments. It can also arise over any type of material, from a document to a house.

Replevin actions arise over public documents that get mixed into someone's papers. For instance, you may have an ancestor who once served as mayor of a town, and some town records wound up in her possession when she left office. The town could initiate a replevin action to reclaim those public documents.

What's a public document? The federal government and each of the fifty states define public documents slightly differently, but all definitions have common themes saying that public documents, regardless of media or characteristics, were (1) made, (2) received, and/or (3) maintained by a government agency to document the transaction of its official business. Examples of public documents include the official business records of cities and towns, such as the charters or records of organizations; the documents recorded and retained by municipal

Dana, a dealer in historic documents, received the grandchildren of old Mrs. Laudable in his office. She had died recently, and her descendants had come from a neighboring state to clean out the house so it could go on the market. They brought with them a box of documents they found, wondering if he would like to buy any of them. As Dana expected, most of the contents had historical value but no commercial value. When he unfolded three bundles, he discovered lots of signatures of local citizens who had gained some historical importance within the state. The three bundles represented three different types of documents: letters written to government officials, applications for various government-issued licenses, and reports of activities addressed to and by various government officials. Dana knew state law would regard all of those as public documents.

During the conversation, Dana learned that a member of the Laudable family had served as the local Town Clerk for thirty-five years in the nineteenth century—before the town built a government office building. He had his office in this home, and these public documents did not get moved to the municipal building when it opened. Dana encouraged the Laudables to return the public documents to local government, and to donate the rest to the local historical society.

clerks, such as voter registration records; or the records of government institutions, such as poor farms, jails, public hospitals, and public schools of all sorts.

States generally argue that when public documents fall into private hands, the public has no access to important historical information about the state and the nation. Further, since public documents record government actions, having them in private hands hampers government accountability because the public has no access to them. Many states, although not all, specifically forbid the private ownership of public documents.

The use of replevin in relation to public documents has increased in the last decade or two, largely because media programs like *Antiques Road Show* have increased the public's awareness of the monetary value of some historical documents. Further, Internet-based auction sites, like eBay, and "classified ad" services, like Craigslist, have dramatically increased the public's ability to sell historical documents.

SPOILS OF WAR AND CULTURAL TREASURES PROTECTION

On the philosophy that wars come and go but that a people's cultural heritage should survive across time, a series of international laws forbid combatants from collecting or destroying the cultural treasures and artifacts they find in an enemy country. A variety of laws protecting cultural treasures against looting and destruction during violent conflicts first appeared during the nineteenth century. They established laws against looting or destruction of cultural treasures, heritage institutions, and private papers during war.

The trend started with the Brussels Declaration of 1874.[2] It was followed by the Hague Conventions of 1899 and 1907, the Roerich Pact, the Hague Convention of 1954 (Hague, 1954), and UNESCO Convention of 1970.[3] All attempt to establish the concept that military victory should take second place to the protection of cultural objects, and that the theft and trafficking in cultural property is illegal. These agreements have received very little support in practice, but the US government has signed them, and so cultural repositories keep an eye out for incoming items that may fall under them.

If an ancestor picked up an enemy helmet or gun and brought it home as a souvenir, no law applies. If the same ancestor brought home some jewelry found in an unguarded museum or diaries found in a home or unguarded archives, the law applies. As with Native American antiquities and wildlife parts, you cannot do much with the spoils of war without attracting legal attention, and a museum will probably balk if you offer the spoils to them. If you know where the spoils came from, consider sending them back to the country of origin. Contact the country's consulate to find out the process.

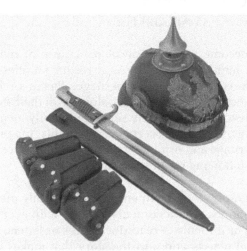

A German military pickelhaube helmet, bayonet, and cartridge pouch—souvenirs, now considered spoils of war.

As part of a US Army infantry unit stationed in the Pacific Theater during World War II, Gerald, an accomplished trumpet musician, was a member of a service band. These bands performed when required and functioned as stretcher bearers when needed. As a stretcher bearer one day, Gerald picked up a multiple-page letter lying beside the corpse of a dead Japanese soldier. The document, written in Japanese on a long, narrow sheet paper, contained some drawings. Gerald took the letter home with him when the war ended. The letter stayed in a cedar chest along with Gerald's war medals, uniforms, and other mementoes for seventy years until his son, Garret, cleaned out the family home. Garret had heard about the letter years before but had forgotten about its existence. By the time he came across it, the letter had become very fragile. Garret took it to a university foreign language department, where he learned that the writer had written the letter using a writing system of characters that changed after the war ended, and the current faculty couldn't read it. Garret looked for someone versed in the older writing to translate it. As people became aware of the letter and its history, someone raised the "spoils of war" issue. Did the laws governing them apply to this letter? Probably. Garret decided he would return the letter to the family of the Japanese soldier if his name could be deciphered and the family found. If that proved impossible, he would donate the letter to a museum.

AVAILABILITY

Today's families can become very complicated because of remarriages and assorted blended family structures. As a result, families face the fragmentation of their collective family heritage. Pieces of historical documents, papers, objects, and photographs, along with their stories and views of the family's history, go to widely separated family members. To retain the history, someone should accept responsibility for preserving the collective family heritage and bring together disparate pieces to create a cohesive whole. The following suggestions may help.

- Photocopy photographs and documents for each family member.
- Scan or print out photos and documents to share with everyone.
- Transcribe special or difficult-to-read documents or letters.
- Photograph special objects and add the story that makes it significant.
- Interview members of the family to make an oral history.
- Ask family members to write their life history to add to your documents.
- Store what you have in archival-quality notebooks, photograph albums, folders, and/or boxes.
- Prepare your materials as a print-on-demand book through an online service, making the access link available to family members so anyone can purchase a bound copy of what you put together.
- Provide each claimant with a copy of the contents, but not the original documents.
- Resist the notion of dividing up the artifacts; the division will fragment the family history.
- If you digitize your records, make sure that you (1) preserve those digital records and (2) preserve the original paper copies. Consider donating them to a repository so everyone has equal access to them.

Lorraine belonged to a large family. She had dozens of first cousins, and hundreds of second cousins, nieces, and nephews. After the last of her own six children left home, she got interested in the family genealogy and uncovered a wide variety of documents that she systematically copied and filed. As she cleaned out her own attic, Lorraine insisted that her grown children had a say in what she did with their materials—report cards, school photos, their letters home from school and camp, and objects or collections left in the attic. If they wanted them, they took them. If they did not, Lorraine added them to the collection. When she had gone as far as she could go with her research, Lorraine gave a copy of specific documents to everyone who asked for something, and then she donated her complete collection to the local historical society, which received it gladly.

By placing her work in a repository, Lorraine assured that the material would stay together in a safe environment, making it available to future generations and historical researchers alike.

The designated family historian brings together all of the tangible materials to create a cohesive collection available to everyone.

FAMILY SECRETS, PRIVATE MATTERS, AND PRIVACY

Somewhere in the family tree, every family has an issue involving privacy, private matters, or family secrets. It may happen that you discover a cache of letters or a diary discussing money, mental illness, poor decisions, or shameful or criminal behavior, such as excessive drinking, infidelity, domestic violence, child abuse, politically and socially offensive attitudes, and so on. As with all personal materials, regardless of how shocking, painful, or embarrassing, it has historical value. If you have the impulse to throw away the materials to protect the privacy of the people involved, or other family members, from the knowledge of these relatives' behaviors, please resist it.

Revealing family secrets of the recent past can actually have a therapeutic effect on family members. In the words of Bruce Feiler, "Some things are too painful to discuss while people are living but too important to be left unsaid after they die."[4] In his *New York Times* article, he recounts the story of a few people who pursued the truth about a family secret—some even wrote books about the process and the results—and came to a positive outcome.[5] The truth will indeed set us free.

Family secrets can reveal (1) motives for people's actions as they work to protect a previously unknown secret, (2) hidden connections between one person and another or between a person and an event, and (3) the genuine community mores of the day and the perspective of people in the process of going against them.

In other words, good private information makes history cleaner and more accurate. A researcher will use the behavior or attitude captured in your materials to support a point while minimizing references to the actual people involved.

In early October 2013, members of a listserv for archivists discussed how they would explain the historical value of "dirty laundry." Participants offered the following thoughts:

> By preserving [the documents,] the dirty laundry can be understood in the larger context of whatever happened, minimizing the negative reaction. If the record is altered or destroyed and people find out, history may judge someone more harshly because the complete facts aren't available, or they have to be reconstructed from (possibly biased or hostile) outside sources. At the very least [the story] goes from "They did something -iffy" to "They did something -iffy and then they tried to hide it; who knows what else they did and destroyed papers about?" Kind of a "tell the truth and you won't get in more trouble than you deserve" sort of argument.[6]

> If we just cherry-pick what is donated about a family or individual the future will not possibly have a full understanding of the past. Dirty-laundry reflects something unpleasant, but it also reflects something that really happened. And if history is to be truthful, all of it is needed.[7]

> Donations of other individuals to other institutions might contain documents on the same dirty-laundry [incident]. Perhaps the donor would prefer that his/her/their take on whatever is preserved to reflect his/her/their side of the situation.[8]

It all comes down to this point: "Sanitized history is fiction."[9] The histori-cal record needs all the laundry—clean and dirty—it can get.

Today we understand the causes and manifestations of post-traumatic stress disorder (PTSD), but our understanding came out of the 1970s as the medical profession studied soldiers returning from the war in Vietnam. Before then, we referred to soldiers as suffering from "battle fatigue," "shell shock," or "soldier's heart," but didn't look much deeper than that. Now that we understand trauma-driven behavior, historians want to apply that understanding to the aftermath of wars and national disasters, such as the Johnstown Flood (1889), the San Francisco Earth-quake (1906), and the Chicago Fire (1871). Where would they look? Court records and newspaper accounts, of course, but PTSD-driven behavior in the nineteenth century probably would not become so public. The best information would come from diaries and letters in which people con-fided the pain, fear, sadness, and general chaos in their lives or the life of a loved one. The historian will focus on the behavior without making moral judgments about the people or their families.

As well as traumatic incidents, private matters can also include positive behavior, such as the private adoption of a child or the anonymous finan-cial support for a cause that was controversial at the time—like women's suffrage, abortion, or gay rights.

Regardless of the behavior that someone wants to hide in the present, the behavior contributed to real life in the time and place, and so making it available will have value to those trying to understand an aspect of that life. Societies have a very hard time developing an understanding of the details of everyday life long ago. Researchers find much about the surface of existence in most letters and diaries, but a complete picture requires full access to private matters and family secrets.

A different form of family secret involves public scandal. If it happened in the past, current family members may not know about it, even though contemporary materials document it reliably.

The Fuller family found they had a collection of several boxes of letters, ledgers, notebooks, a few photographs, and some objects, such as keys, glasses, and ashtrays, after the deaths of several el-derly family members. Most of the materials came from the family hotel business during the 1920s and early 1930s in East Tennessee. The hotel itself had been sold out of the family and burned in the 1970s. The current generations had not seen much of the collected material because, for decades the Fuller patriarchs and matriarchs would not talk about certain aspects of the family history, hinting of some sort of public scandal and unseemly conduct. When the current generations finally read and examined what they had, the truth came out. The family had indeed owned a hotel in town during Prohibition (1920–1933), which included an illegal bootlegging operation and speakeasy. The Dixie Highway, which stretched from Michigan to Florida and was a major route for the cross-border transport of large quantities of illegal liquor, ran near their East Tennessee town. The Fuller family employed "bootleggers" on that route to bring alcohol to their hotel. The newspaper clippings in the collection even suggested the Fullers were linked to Al Capone, a major mobster based in Chicago. Their speakeasy occupied a block of rooms on the north side of the hotel "reserved" for special trusted guests. In it the hotel sold illegal alcoholic beverages in an atmosphere that included music, dancing, and gambling. The post–World War II generation had squelched all information about their parents' business history because they found it embarrassing. Not only was it illegal, they believed it to be immoral. Regardless, the collection of material revealed the family's undeniable past. After a lengthy discussion, current family members recognized the historical value of the materials and decided to offer them to the county archives.

What might seem like a family secret to the current generation was well-known to previous generations. There would be no point in trying to cover it up. Making the private papers of the family available, on the other hand, would greatly enhance the story behind the public reporting on it.

If materials containing details of private matters wind up in a repository, the staff will go to great lengths to protect the privacy of the people involved. People's privacy occupies a fair amount of space in the minds of archivists and curators—especially the privacy of third parties—that is, parties whose letters arrive in a repository in the papers of someone else. The Core Values Statement and Code of Ethics of the Society of American Archivists calls for the protection of the privacy of third parties, and repositories regularly place access restrictions on collections to protect the privacy and confidentiality of the people in the collection, particularly individuals and groups who have no voice or role in a collection's creation, retention, or public use.

The right of privacy does not extend to the dead, however.[10] Therefore, archivists place restrictions on access to materials for lengths of time generally regarded as long enough to assure the death of the people involved in potentially sensitive situations. For example, sensitive materials from a fifty-something donor may have a fifty-year restriction placed on them. That does not mean that all the materials in that collection will lie in the dark for fifty years—only the sensitive materials will.

RESOURCES

Archaeological and Anthropological Materials

The US Department of the Interior provides a list of pertinent laws regarding archaeological and anthropological sites and materials: https://www.doi.gov/museum/laws-and-regulations.

Inheritance

All of the individual states have distinct laws and processes concerning estate planning and probate. Cornell Law School's Legal Information Institute provides links to state statutes on inheritance at https://www.law.cornell.edu/wex/table_probate.

Bogleheads.org provides a list of state probate courts at https://www.bogleheads.org/wiki/List_of_US_state_probate_courts.

Intellectual Property Rights

Peter Hirtle's chart on "Copyright Term and the Public Domain in the United States" at Cornell University Library's Copyright Information Center provides an excellent and succinct summary: https://www.copyright.cornell.edu/publicdomain.

Patent law has an extensive literature. Start with the US Patent and Trademark Office's website at http://www.uspto.gov/patents/resources and branch out from there.

Native American Artifacts

Some museums that have Native American materials or the National Parks Service can help you understand the law and tell you how to go about making a decision about the welfare of your tribal objects. Contact reputable experts and appraisers, perhaps through the Antique Tribal Art Dealers Association (ATADA). Also consider contacting tribal representatives.

Privacy

While the Constitution's Bill of Rights does not specifically mention privacy, in the 1970s Congress began passing specific laws protecting the privacy of financial information, personal identification, and health information. For a general background, the Wikipedia entry at en.wikipedia.org/wiki/Right_to_privacy provides a good introduction.

Replevin

Replevin has not inspired dedicated websites. The best online source we could find appears on Wikipedia at en.wikipedia.org/wiki/Replevin. The only popular book on the topic is Elizabeth H. Dow's *Archivists, Collectors, Dealers, and Replevin: Case Studies on Private Ownership of Public Documents*. Lanham, MD: Scarecrow Press, 2012, which focuses on replevin as it applies to public documents.

NOTES

1. Bankrate, "How Long to Keep Financial Records" (April 10, 2015), www.bankrate.com/finance/personal-finance/how-long-to-keep-financial-records.aspx

2. For a summary of the Brussels Declaration of 1874, see the United States Committee of the Blue Shield (USCBS), http://uscbs.org/1874-brussels-declaration.html. For the full text document of the Brussels Declaration of 1874, see the International Committee of the Red Cross https://ihl-databases.icrc.org/ihl/INTRO/135.

3. For a summary of The Hague Conventions of 1899 and 1907, see the United States Committee of the Blue Shield (USCBS), http://uscbs.org/1899---1907-hague-conventions.html. For the full text of The Hague Convention of 1899, see the International Committee of the Red Cross, https://ihl-databases.icrc.org/ihl/INTRO/150?OpenDocument. For the full text of The Hague Conventions of 1907, see the International Committee of the Red Cross, https://ihl-databases.icrc.org/ihl/INTRO/195. For a summary of the Roerich Pact 1935 see the United States Committee of the Blue Shield (USCBS), http://uscbs.org/1935-roerich-pact.html. For the full text of the Roerich Pact 1935, see the International Committee of the Red Cross, https://ihl-databases.icrc.org/applic/ihl/ihl.nsf/Treaty.xsp?documentId=EE57F295093E44A4C12563CD002D6A3F&action=openDocument. For a summary of The Hague Convention of 1954, see the United Nations Educational, Scientific and Cultural Organization (UNESCO), http://www.unesco.org/new/en/culture/themes/armed-conflict-and-heritage/convention-and-protocols/1954-hague-convention/. For the full text document of The Hague Convention of 1954, see UNESCO, http://portal.unesco.org/en/ev.php-URL_ID=13637&URL_DO=DO_TOPIC&URL_SECTION=201.html. For a summary of the UNESCO Convention of 1970 (Convention on the Means of Prohibiting and Preventing the Illicit Import, Export, and Transfer of Ownership of Cultural Property), see UNESCO, http://www.unesco.org/new/en/culture/themes/

illicit-trafficking-of-cultural-property/1970-convention/. For the full text document of the UNESCO Convention of 1970, see the United Nations Educational, Scientific and Cultural Organization (UNESCO), http://portal.unesco.org/en/ev.php-URL_ID=13039&URL_DO=DO_TOPIC&URL_SECTION=201.html, and http://www.unesco.org/new/en/culture/themes/illicit-trafficking-of-cultural-property/1970-convention/text-of-the-convention/.

4. Bruce Feiler, "Secret Histories," *New York Times*, January 17, 2014, ST1.

5. Michael Hainey, *After Visiting Friends: A Son's Story* (New York: Scribner, 2013); Emma Brockes, *She Left Me the Gun: My Mother's Life Before Me* (New York: Penguin, 2014).

6. Eric Willey, Archives and Archivists listserv (October 3, 2013), forums.archivists.org/read/?forum=archives.

7. Bruce Turner, Archives and Archivists listserv (October 3, 2013), forums.archivists.org/read/?forum=archives.

8. Ibid.

9. Anna Heran, Archives and Archivists listserv, (October 3, 2013), forums.archivists.org/read/?forum=archives.

10. Rebecca Herold, "Is There Privacy beyond Death?" Privacy Guidance (March 2005), www.privacyguidance.com/files/Privacy_Beyond_Death_Herold.pdf.

8

Preserving Your Family Objects and Papers

Everything deteriorates—alas—some items faster than others, depending on the circumstances. Too often we relegate our family heirlooms to attics, basements, or outbuildings where they face destructive temperatures, humidity, pests, and pollutants. Or perhaps we display them near a source of heat, use them to cover a bed in front of a window, or hang them on a wall in the bathroom. To preserve your family's historical papers and objects, you need to understand what causes them to deteriorate.

CAUSES OF DETERIORATION AND DESTRUCTION

Physical Forces: Examples include fast and catastrophic events, such as natural disasters (earthquakes) and human error (bumping or dropping an object), or slower-acting repeated assaults (improper handling during use or vibrations from nearby construction). The risk of deterioration due to physical force appears when artifacts do not have proper support, whether they are on display, in storage, or being moved.

Thieves, Vandals, Displacers: Examples include planned theft by thieves, opportunistic theft by visitors, and vandalism.

Fire: Examples include localized small fires or whole-house fires. Fire can cause the quick and catastrophic loss of a wide variety of materials. Further, the use of water to extinguish fires can lead to extensive damage.

Water: Examples include storage areas in attic or basement spaces vulnerable to leaking roofs or leaking plumbing, sprinkler system malfunctions, or flooding.

Pests: Examples include rodents, insects, mold, mildew, fungi, and the occasional feral animal. While pesticides and fungicides exist, they can damage collections.

Pollutants: Examples include airborne particulates, like soot and dust, or acidic gasses, like formaldehyde. Pollutants can originate both inside and outside of buildings.

Light: Examples include sunlight and full-spectrum artificial lights. Light damage, which is cumulative and irreversible, results from intense light used over a prolonged length of exposure. The same sun that bleaches sheets on a clothesline bleaches pictures on a wall. Ultraviolet light causes the most damage.

Incorrect Temperature: Examples include hot attics and freezing garages. The detrimental effects of temperature kept either too high or too low take a long time to appear, and we may not notice the slow deterioration that results. Heat speeds chemical reactions. For every additional eighteen degrees, chemical reactions approximately double in speed, regardless of the materials. The useful life of paper is cut in half by every increase of ten degrees.

Incorrect Relative Humidity: Examples include damp basements and dry attics. Organic materials all contain moisture; they absorb and give off moisture and try to find a balance between their moisture content and that in the air around them. If the moisture content in the air goes up, they absorb moisture and swell. If it goes down, they give off moisture and shrink. If this cycle occurs slowly and moderately, no damage occurs. However, sudden, large, and frequent fluctuations in relative humidity can cause shrinkage, warping, splitting, and general aging of objects made of organic materials. A sudden increase in moisture content can cause condensation on metal artifacts and will promote corrosion.

Custodial Neglect: Examples include poor housekeeping, rough handling, and improper storage. Custodial neglect occurs when materials do not receive active care to preserve them. It also occurs when the care follows inaccurate information and bad practices.

In summary, preservation means doing what will prolong the life of historically valuable materials.

CAREFUL HANDLING = PRESERVATION

- Always have a clean area, clean hands, and clean materials.
- Have no food or drink nearby, and don't smoke.
- Don't use rubber bands, tape, glue, paper clips, or other fasteners. Instead, use pencils—which can be erased—folders, envelopes, and boxes.
- Handle each item as little as possible, and treat it as if it were precious.
- Carry three-dimensional objects with both hands to support them, and prepare a place for putting them down before you pick them up.
- Curators and archivists use gloves when working with historical photographs (but not documents) and objects, and you may wish to

also. Use clean gloves for photographs and disposable synthetic rubber (nitrile) gloves when working with slippery surface objects such as glass, ceramics, and metal.

- Resist the urge to fix it, even if it's broken. Taping a torn photo, gluing a broken vase, wiping a smudged painting, stripping a tabletop all actually do more damage than good. Contact an expert or professional conservator to restore or repair your valued items.
- Buy supplies like polypropylene envelopes from a reputable archival supply dealer.
- If something needs cleaning, follow the least harmful route. Dust it or brush off surface dirt, remove it from a frame, or wipe it dry; otherwise leave it alone. Don't dry clean historical fabrics.

Old materials can be dirty and dusty. If you found them stored in a damp, humid environment, they may also contain mold, mildew, bacteria, and sometimes chemicals. Old mold and fresh mold can both present health problems, therefore keep books, papers, and other items that you suspect of having mold isolated in a box or container and consider asking a professional for assistance if you think the material might have value. You may also consider photocopying or digitizing documents and then printing paper copies.

Take precautions when you handle dirty or suspect objects and materials. (1) Wear gloves, either plastic or cotton, and wear something over your clothes—an old shirt, apron, or lab coat. (2) Work in a well-ventilated area, perhaps with a dust mask or handkerchief over your face. (3) When you have finished working with dirty, dusty, or moldy materials, change your clothes and wash them, then wash your hands with soap and water. Following basic commonsense guidelines will help prevent you from having potentially harmful health problems.

ORGANIZATION = PRESERVATION

Organizing your historically significant materials will help protect them from damage and loss.

- Conduct an inventory of the items you think may have historic value. For each item, or group of items, include the location of the item in your house or storage area, the condition of the item, who made it, the date of the item, who purchased it, date of purchase, what material(s) it is made of, who owned it, and the story of the object and why it is important. It is also wise to photograph each item and place a copy of the photograph and inventory sheet with the object so that its story will accompany it.

- If you don't have time right now to undertake a detailed inventory, at least find the items, write down what they are, inspect them, and if you think they face immediate danger, place them in a container or move them to a safe place.
- Keep your inventory up to date. Note any changes in location when you move something or let someone borrow it. Be diligent about following up on the object's return. Many heirlooms have been lost in other people's care.

You may find yourself having to sort through vast amounts of things to find historically significant ones. While daunting and overwhelming, it can be done. Don't despair. Line up bins, boxes, and containers and start sorting through items, grouping like items together. All the jewelry goes in one container, all the photographs in another, all the linens in another. Designate one bin for objects you think might have historical value. If you have papers, don't separate them. Part of their value lies in their context, where they came from, who wrote them, and the stories they tell. Keep papers together as you found them so you don't destroy the context of one document to another. Use as many containers as you need, and label each of them. After a while, you will have finished sorting and can begin to deal with the distribution of the contents in each container.

APPROPRIATE HOUSING AND STORAGE = PRESERVATION

Housing and storing your historically significant objects in archival materials and environmentally controlled conditions will greatly prolong their life.

- As a general rule, wrap objects and/or separate them with either acid-free paper or tissue or with washed cotton or muslin. Do not use plastic bags, cardboard, Styrofoam, regular tissue paper, or wood. They all contain ingredients—usually acid—which speeds up the deterioration of things stored in them.
- After individually wrapping each of the pieces, house them in acid-free or inert containers that will not harm them further.
- Store material in a clean, dry, cool area that has good airflow and a controlled temperature. The best setting for both people and materials is a temperature of 64°F–72°F, with a relative humidity of about 45–55 percent.
- Store objects and documents away from radiators and vents.
- Keep objects and papers away from direct light—especially textiles, paper, watercolors, photographic images, and natural history specimens.

- Store hanging clothing with padded hangers to prevent stress and creases. Roll large flat textiles like quilts and flags onto large tubes. If the tube is acidic cardboard, cover the tube with acid-free paper or cotton sheeting. Store folded textiles with the least number of creases and folds possible.
- Keep photographs in acid-free and lignin-free protective sleeves or enclosures made of paper or a plastic that you can't smell, such as uncoated polyester, polyethylene, and polypropylene. Store them in acid-free boxes or archival-quality albums. Avoid albums with "magnetic" or "no stick" colored pages. They can harm photographs over time.
- Store family papers and documents in acid-free folders or polyester film enclosures in flat boxes or vertical file or document boxes. Remove metal fasteners, and paper clips.
- If you have a separate storage area with lots of boxes or crates, keep it clean and free of pests. Place boxes on shelves or pallets at least three inches off the floor to prevent water damage from minor flooding. If you stack boxes, stack them no more than three boxes high with the heaviest boxes on the bottom. Do not put anything directly under water pipes that could leak or in areas that could flood.
- If you live in an area subject to extreme and dangerous weather, consider boxing the most important items in your family inventory separately. Label the box and place it where you can get to it quickly when an emergency arises. You will be glad you did.
- Have appropriate fire extinguishers and smoke detector/alarms in various areas of your house, and know how to use them.
- Watch out for air pollutants and contaminants that can damage objects in storage areas. Many of these pollutants, such as smoke (tobacco and wood), soot, dirt and dust, auto emissions, acidic gasses, and particulates hurt people as well. To minimize the damage from such pollutants, keep your house clean, replace air intake filters on HVAC systems regularly, eliminate dust and outside contaminants from entering by caulking and weather stripping windows and doors, use door mats, and store artifacts in appropriate enclosed containers.
- If you find pests in storage areas—insects, rodents, mold, or mildew—trap or remove them as organically as possible. Avoid using toxic chemicals such as pesticides or fungicides, mothballs, and such. Since prevention is always best, prevent pest entry by installing or repairing building structures or entryways, removing food from areas, improving climate control, and keeping areas clean.

PROPER HOME DISPLAY = PRESERVATION

Properly displaying your historically significant materials will prevent them from deteriorating or becoming faded or damaged. Display objects or documents in a part of the house away from direct light and moisture. Consider having paper, photographs, or two-dimensional artwork framed or prepared by a professional who will use acid-free materials and spacers so that the piece does not touch the glass or glazing. Display other objects in secure, clean, and nonacidic materials. If you hang textiles, fully support them to reduce the pull of gravity. Display three-dimensional objects on their most stable side and avoid placing breakable objects where they might be knocked off or fall due to vibrations.

Digital Materials

Electronic devices have drastically changed the environment that shapes our archival collections.[1] The concept of "personal" has become much larger, with fuzzier boundaries than when everything depended on paper. The term *papers* no longer refers to just documents.[2] The electronic and social media network of people's lives have become both wider and more complicated than in the pre-electronic world. Social media "conversations" may have historical value, and we hope you can save them.

Be prepared to find electronic materials everywhere on a wide variety of electronic storage media. Understand that saving them means giving them lots of tender loving care throughout their lifetime. All hazards, from a faulty electrical system to a natural disaster, threaten digital materials far more than they threaten artifacts and paper-based collections.

To preserve your family's digital "papers," start by preserving the storage media that hold them. Convert as much as you can to a stable paper format by printing both text and image documents. After the conversion, you can put the materials into a box, put the box on a shelf, keep it cool and in the dark, and expect them to last for decades, if not centuries. Unfortunately, some electronic materials, such as databases, sound recordings, webpages, and so on, do not convert to paper. You must keep them electronically.

While you have digital materials on old media, "refresh" them periodically by "playing" them—that is, putting them into the electronic environment that created them and in which their creators intended them to work. Refreshing will preserve digital materials for a while, but eventually both the hardware and the storage media will die. Before that happens, you must migrate the materials to a new environment.

Migration means copying digital materials from an old storage media to a new one. The new storage media will be either of the same type as before, for example, hard drive to hard drive; or a different type, such as a floppy disc to a flash drive. You may already have experienced copying the content of 5.25" floppy discs to 3.5" floppy discs and then to CDs. Not much changes, because you simply re-created the file in another place.

However, if you have ever reformatted a word-processed file to a different format, say .doc to .rtf, you know that the file changes a lot. Reformatting produces another version of the document; it does not re-create the original.

To minimize the loss of data as files age, reformat all documents of a particular type to a single, open-source file format—it's called normalizing. For instance, if you have WordPerfect .wpd files and a variety of Microsoft Word .doc and .docx files, you could normalize them all as Open Office .odt files that everything can read.

In sum, to keep your digital materials across time, convert as much as you can to paper. If you have materials you can't convert to paper, at least do the following:

- Normalize all file types to a single open-source file type.
- Migrate everything onto a hard drive or dedicated backup drive at least every two years. Make a paper copy of the directory of your drive and store it with the drive.
- Refresh everything at least every two years.
- Every five years or so the technology will have changed, so you will need to migrate everything to a new backup drive.
- The gold standard: Save three copies of everything in three different media and store them in three different geographic locations that do not suffer the same natural disasters.

A stable environment and regular housekeeping will substantially reduce environmental threats to your material. However, as we rely on trained doctors to look after our illnesses, we recommend you leave the treatment or repair of damaged objects or documents to a conservator or other professional trained to address the problems. Fortunately, many books and websites describe how to preserve various types of materials that you might encounter in your attic.

RESOURCES

American Institute for Conservation. This organization serves professionals who specialize in the conservation of three-dimensional artifacts.

You will find the "Find a Conservator" pages especially useful. http://www.conservation-us.org.

Fisher, Charles E., and Hugh C. Miller (eds.). *Caring for Your Historic House*. New York: Harry N. Abrams, 1998. A guide developed by Heritage Preservation and the National Park Service on how to care for historic houses.

Image Permanence Institute. *Stored Alive*. This tool turns the interacting aspects of preservation into a game. https://www.imagepermanenceinstitute.org/resources/stored-alive.

Image Permanence Institute. *Dew Point Calculator*. This tool makes figuring out how to set your climate controls easy. https://www.imagepermanenceinstitute.org/resources/dew-point-calculator.

Landry, Gregory, et al. *The Winterthur Guide to Caring for Your Collection*. Winterthur, DE: The Henry Francis DuPont Winterthur Museum, Inc, 2000. Another overview of caring for collections emphasizing antiques.

Library of Congress. *Personal Archiving, Preserving Your Digital Memories*. This extensive website explains the preservation of all types of personal digital documents from photos to movies to email. It includes videos and many how-to resources. https://www.digitalpreservation.gov/personalarchiving.

Library of Congress, The American Folklife Center. Resources for Family Folklife and History. This portal contains links to a wide variety of resources on the care of archival material. https://www.loc.gov/folklife/familyfolklife/resources.html.

Long, Jane S., and Richard W. Long. *Caring for Your Family Treasures: Heritage Preservation*. New York: Harry N. Abrams, Inc. A book written by conservators to assist families and family curators in caring for family belongings.

Northeast Document Conservation Center. *Preservation 101 Online*. This online textbook covers the preservation of paper collections and related formats, including how to identify deteriorated materials, how to properly care for collections, and how to set priorities for conservation action. https://nedcc.org/preservation101/welcome.

Northeast Document Conservation Center. *Preservation Leaflets*. A wealth of free online pamphlets on all aspects of the preservation of historical materials. https://www.nedcc.org/free-resources/preservation-leaflets/overview.

Ogden, Sherelyn, ed. (2004) *Caring for American Indian Objects: A Practical and Cultural Guide*. St. Paul: Minnesota Historical Society Press. The authoritative source on the care of American Indian artifacts.

Paradigm. *Guidelines for Creators of Personal Archives*. Practical advice anyone can implement to maximize the chances that your digital ma-

terial will survive for as long as you need it. http://www.paradigm
.ac.uk/workbook/appendices/guidelines-tips.html.

Paradigm. *Useful Resources for Digital Preservation Strategies.* A bibliogra-
phy of strategies for preserving digital materials. http://www.para
digm.ac.uk/workbook/introduction/useful-resources.html.

Quye, Anita, and Colin Williamson (eds.). *Plastics: Collection and Conserving.* Edinburgh: NMS Publishing Limited, 1999. One of the few
books on the care of plastic materials of all types.

Redwine, Gabriella, et al. *Born Digital: Guidance for Donors, Dealers,
and Archival Repositories (CLIR Publication No. 159).* Washington, DC:
Council on Library and Information Resources, 2013. Highly authoritative recommendations on the handling and preservation of digital
materials. https://www.clir.org/pubs/reports/pub159.

Ritzenthaler, Mary Lynn. 2010. *Preserving Archives and Manuscripts.*
Second edition. Chicago: Society of American Archivists. The authoritative resource on the preservation of archives, manuscripts,
and historical collections.

Ritzenthaler, Mary Lynn, and Diane L. Vogt-O'Connor, with Helena
Zinkham, Brett Carnell, and Kit A. Peterson. *Photographs: Archival
Care and Management.* Chicago: Society of American Archivists, 2006.
The authoritative and pragmatic guide to all aspects of managing
photographic collections.

Williams, Don, and Louisa Jaggar. *Saving Stuff: How to Care for and
Preserve Your Collectibles, Heirlooms and Other Prized Possessions.* New
York: Simon and Schuster, 2005. A book full of practical advice on
the care of family belongings written by the former senior conserva-
tor of furniture at the Smithsonian Institution's Center for Materials
Research and Education.

Suppliers of Archival Materials

Archival Products, P.O. Box 1413, Des Moines, IA 50306-1413. https://
www.archival.com.

Conservation Resources International, LLC, 5532 Port Royal Road,
Springfield, VA 22151. http://www.conservationresources.com.

Gaylord Bros., PO Box 4901, Syracuse, NY 13221-4901. http://www.gay
lord.com.

Hollinger Metal Edge, 6340 Bandini Blvd., Commerce, CA 90040 or
9401 Northeast Dr. Fredericksburg, VA 22408. http://www.hollinger
metaledge.com.

MASTERPAK, 145 East 57th Street, 5th Floor, New York, NY 10022.
http://www.masterpak-usa.com.

Tru Vue, Inc., 9400 W. 55th Street, McCook, IL 60525. https://www.
tru-vue.com.
University Products Inc., 517 Main Street, Holyoke, MA 01040. https://
www.universityproducts.com.

NOTES

1. Elizabeth H. Dow, *Electronic Records in the Manuscript Repository* (Lanham, MD: Scarecrow Press, 2009).
2. Tom Hyry and Rachel Onuf, "The Personality of Electronic Records: The Impact of New Information Technology on Personal Papers." *Archival Issues: Journal of the Midwest Archives Conference* 22, no. 1: 39–41.

9

Donating Your Family Objects and Papers

No matter how carefully you work to preserve your family artifacts and documents, there may come a time when (1) you need to get rid of objects and archives and/or (2) nobody in the family wants the responsibility of caring for them. When that happens, consider placing the collection in a repository.

We repeat: Cultural institutions—museums, archives, historical societies, historic houses, libraries, art galleries, and so on—guard our historical evidence. They exist to preserve documents and objects so we can understand the past and how things have changed over time—it's their job. Some of those materials come from governments, but many come from families or businesses. Family collections contain much surprising and insightful information that may not appear anywhere else about a person, a group, a town, or a community.

With your materials in a repository, all members of your family will have access to them, and so will historians who will use them to tell a unique story or add more detail to ongoing research. If your family's materials are lost, split up, or thrown away, none of that can happen—the family story will become distorted, or it will completely disappear. Before you send your documents to a repository you make digital scans of everything and print them onto archival paper, with, perhaps, a transcription, so everyone can have a set, while the originals go to a repository. The repository will ensure that many generations from now the family still has access to its history. Unfortunately, that does not work for artifacts. One person will get the real thing, and everyone else will get a picture of it.

Historical repositories collect materials that reflect their particular missions. Museums collect objects; archives collect documents; some historical societies collect both. Historical museums and archives evaluate materials on the basis of their historical use to that museum. When offered materials for their collections, archivists and curators choose materials that have enough value to make them worth caring for permanently, as we emphasize in chapters 3–6. This evaluation activity vexes curators and

Consider placing your historically significant family artifacts and documents in a historical repository, such as an archive, museum, or historical society.

archivists more than any other professional duty. If they make a wrong decision, either they leave a hole in the fabric of history or they fill their shelves with materials of little use to their public.

However, while both museums and archives have many similarities, they also have many differences.

MUSEUMS

Museums hold collections of artifacts with the intention of holding those collections forever and making them available for education and research. The collections reflect the interests expressed by the organization's members. Some focus on art, others on science, natural history, or human history, and thus, those museums store, care for, exhibit, and interpret representative objects that typify those specializations. In general, museums offer a way to see and, sometimes, to feel objects from the past.

Museums usually have a mission statement and a collecting policy that describes the parameters of their collections. Most museums refer newly offered objects or collections to an acquisitions committee that decides whether the offer suits the museum's focus and whether the museum has the space and ability to care for the offered collection. Since museum objects can take up so much more room than the type of materials an archives collects, *museums tend to be highly selective about what they accept.* A museum may decline something because it already has examples; it needs only so many high school mascot plush toys or vintage typewriters—regardless of how good the condition is or who owned it.

Museums usually have much larger collections than they can exhibit at any one time. Continual display causes objects to deteriorate. Thus, in order to fulfill their mission of preserving their collections forever, museums rotate their exhibits and move objects in and out of storage. The objects in most museums receive attentive care even while in the deep recesses of storage.

Regardless of focus, museums usually have three types of collections: (1) the main collection intended for exhibition and study, (2) an education collection intended for hands-on activities with items that can be used up, and (3) a prop collection of items used as props for exhibits.

Museums take very seriously their mandate to use their collections to educate, so they mount exhibits and make their collections available to scholars and the public for research purposes. Unlike the relatively formal and prescribed learning of a classroom, a museum educates in an informal manner—so informal that visitors may not even realize that they have learned anything. Museums offer visitors a chance to investigate stories in a visual way. They make it possible for visitors to understand points that a written work would not convey as well. In addition to exhibitions, museums also offer programming, community events, and classes for children, adults, and families.

ARCHIVES

Like museums, archives usually have a mission statement and a collecting policy that describes the parameters of their collections. When someone offers them materials, the staff will consider whether the collection falls within the archives' mission statement, whether it has enough historical usefulness to earn the space it will fill, and whether the archives has the space and resources to care for it.

The archivist expects to hold those collections forever, making them available for education and research. Although most archives have a geographically determined focus, such as the National Archives, state historical societies, or local historical societies, a few have also developed a specialization in particular types of material, such as literary collections, political collections, or artists' collections. Some specialize in a particular era or event, such as World War I and World War II museums and holocaust museums.

Archives provide researchers access to their holdings, but unlike a library where patrons may browse through the books the library holds, archives, to protect their unique holdings, do not allow patrons to examine anything at random. Instead, the staff arrange and describe a collection and develop guides, called finding aids, that allow researchers to review the content without actually handling the materials. When a researcher finds something in a guide he or she wants to see, an archivist retrieves the specific items. The fact that archivists refer to their patrons as "researchers" says a lot about the role they see for the archives.

A researcher working in an archive.

Many families amass collections of documents that are passed down through the generations. After a century or more, these family archives can become quite large and can reflect the lives of a large number of people. Such a collection of family documents will have historical value, and you can probably find an archive that will accept it.

Here's how to go about donating your material to a repository.

Step 1: Describe What You Have

Describing what you have serves three purposes. First, it clarifies for you what you want to donate. Second, it helps you understand where it belongs. Third, it gives any repository you contact a clear understanding of what you're offering. Thus, before approaching a repository about family materials, collect the information they will need to make their decisions and to develop records about your donation.

The archives or museum that receives your family materials will create records for its staff to document what they have, why they have it, where they got it, and where they keep it. They will also create records for the public that provide a context for anyone who uses the collections, including the repository as it creates exhibits. Without information from you, the collections have little or no context about a family, a town, or a region. The stories and supporting information you provide enrich the researchers' and visitors' understanding of your family and the times and places that created the materials.

DESCRIBING ARCHIVES

The Society of American Archivists (SAA) has created a description standard that archivists use when they write up biographical or, in the case of an organization or business, administrative and historical information.[1] We used their lists of information points below, and we recommend that you supply this information as fully as you can. We understand that you may not have details about all of these topics, but gather as much as you can about the person(s), family(ies), and/or corporate body(ies) that created the collections.

For individuals include:

- Names, including the full name, title(s), married name(s), alias(es), pseudonym(s), and common or popular name(s) each person used.
- Where the person lived and the length of residence in each place. Include any other place with which the person had a connection.
- Information about the education or schooling, formal or otherwise, that is important to understanding a person's life.
- The person's principal occupation(s) and career or lifework. Include social status where you can.
- Any other activities important to an understanding of the person's life.
- Significant accomplishments or achievements, including honors, decorations, and noteworthy public recognition.
- Important relationships with other people or organizations and indicate any leadership activities.
- Any other important information not included elsewhere, including family lore or family stories about the individual.

- In all the above, include dates, especially dates of birth and death. If you don't have solid dates, estimate years and decades as closely as you can.

For example:

George Hamilton Bickford was born on October 19, 1868, in Barton, Vermont, to George H. Bickford and Abigail B. (Giffin) Bickford. His father, a Methodist minister, died less than a year later. His mother took her three children to Keene, New Hampshire, where she ran a boarding house. Later she moved to Montpelier, Vermont, where she became a teacher at the Montpelier Seminary.

George received his early education in the public schools of Keene, New Hampshire and graduated from the Montpelier Seminary, followed by Wesleyan University in Middletown, Connecticut. There, he graduated second in his class in 1891, Phi Beta Kappa with honors in history and English literature. He took a job at Haverford College, Haverford, Pennsylvania, as an instructor. He followed that with a brief career as a book salesman. In 1894, he married Alice Holden and went to work for John Stedman Holden, her father, owner of the Bennington textile mill.

Holden invested in a promising granite quarry in Woodbury, Vermont and a small railroad that carried the stone from the quarry to the cutting sheds in Hardwick, Vermont. In 1898, Holden sent Bickford to Hardwick to serve as general manager and treasurer of the Woodbury Granite Company and treasurer for the Hardwick and Woodbury Railroad.

Under Bickford's leadership, the Woodbury Granite Company grew from a small shop with only a half-dozen employees to a giant in the building granite industry. They had two major offices (located in Hardwick, Vermont and New York City), six quarries producing trademarked granite (located in Woodbury and Bethel, Vermont), three large cutting plants (located in Hardwick, Bethel, and Northfield, Vermont), crews working in a dozen cities simultaneously, and over twelve hundred employees. Bickford understood the virtues of vertical integration (the control of every aspect of a business), which allowed him fulfill project schedules at a predictable profit.

Bickford served as the major salesman for his company. A large (six feet, two inches), handsome, energetic, and gregarious man—a champion debater in his academic years—he met people easily and effectively sold the goods and services his company provided to some of the most prominent leaders and families in the country.

Bickford knew how to talk to architects, the key decision makers, not only about architecture but also about art and culture.

A fervent Methodist and staunch Republican, he pursued his business interests aggressively but ethically. For instance, he grew increasingly unhappy with the lending practices of the Hardwick Bank and Trust Company, so, in 1912 he founded and served as president of the Hardwick Granite Bank. He also condemned price-gouging landlords who took advantage of scarce housing for his workers.

The Bickfords and Holdens generously supported the town of Hardwick, providing a substantial amount of support for the local hospital, named for John S. Holden after his death in 1907, and a new building for municipal offices. Bickford died of appendicitis and peritonitis on June 3, 1914, at the Holden Hospital. He left his wife, sons George Floyd and Holden Burr, and daughter Barbara. He is buried in the Holden Family Mausoleum in Bennington, Vermont. At his death, obituaries and editorials across the state and the industry described him as a man of great vision, persuasion, business acumen, and character. The Vermont Republican Party had considered running him for governor.

For families, include:

- Information about the origins of the family and the names of family members, including the facts of marriages, the names of children, and any changes in the family surname or surname spelling.
- Geographical place(s) of residence of the family and the length of residence in each place, as well as any other place with which the family has a connection.
- Information about the formal education or schooling of members of the family.
- The principal activities and occupations of families or their members. Indicate any other activities important to an understanding of the life of the family.
- Significant accomplishments or achievements, including collective honors, decorations, and noteworthy public recognition.
- Describe any familial relationships that have a bearing on understanding the family as a whole.
- Record any other important information not recorded elsewhere.
- In all the above, include dates, especially dates of birth and death. If you don't have solid dates, estimate years and decades as closely as you can.

For example:

> The Lavertu family in Quebec traces its roots back to Jean Guillaume Perron dit Lavertu (1730–1809). Born in Avignon, France, Jean Guillaume joined the French army and arrived in Quebec in 1755. A mason by trade, he participated in the building and repair of a number of forts during and after the French and Indian War. He married eighteen-year-old Marie Josette Allaire in 1757, at St. Joachim. They had ten children.
>
> In 1762, Lavertu had a farm in St.-Francis-de-Sales-de la Riviere-du-Sud. In 1766, he acquired more land on the Etchemin River, south of St.-Henri (today St.-Jean Chrysostome). It became the family homestead. He continued to work as a mason, being involved with building or repairing several parish churches.
>
> The Vermont line descended through Louis, the second son of Jean Guillaume and Josette. Louis married Marie Vermette and fathered fifteen children between 1785 and 1807. At age nineteen, the oldest son, also Louis, married Genevieve Dagneau dit Laprise in 1805. He and his wife received the family homestead.
>
> The Lavertu family multiplied greatly throughout the nineteenth century. Some branches moved toward western Canada, others to the Eastern Townships of Quebec, and yet others into Maine. The part that became the Vermont line generally remained in the area of St. Henri/St.-Jean Chrysostome, Quebec until the twentieth century.
>
> In 1925, Joseph Lavertu (1903–1975), moved from St. Justine, Quebec, to work for Omer Fortin (1875–1974), who had immigrated to Greensboro, Vermont from St. Justine in 1920. Fortin, a blacksmith, had bought a farm that Joseph worked. In 1926, Joseph Lavertu married Marie-Ange Fortin (1904–1967). In 1932, Fortin sold the farm, and Lavertu went into business as a carpenter in Greensboro. By 1939, he had become a contractor, and he moved his family to Hardwick, Vermont.
>
> Joseph and Marie-Ange had eight children: Clermont Marc, called Joe (1926–1994); Lorraine Rose (1928–); Jeannine Marguerite (1929–2013); Francis Lillian (1931–1931); Constance Jacqueline (1932–1970); Paul Norbert (1934–2013); Marie Louise (1935–); and Andrea Simone, called Toby, (1937–).

For businesses or other corporate bodies, include:

- Information relevant to the understanding of the founder's functions, activities, and relations with other businesses. Include the name(s), dates of existence, main functions or activities, and geographic location(s) of the business.

- Date and place of the founding of the business, and if applicable, the date and place of its dissolution.
- Location of the head office and of any branch or regional offices, as well as the geographic region in which the organization operated.
- Include any legal information about incorporation, partnerships, responsibilities, influence of the organization, and the area of activities, including any changes in those legal agreements.
- Include information about the functions and activities of the business.
- Describe the leadership, any changes in leadership, mergers or takeovers, and anything that produced significant changes in the business, including any relationship with predecessor or successor businesses.
- Name all leaders and players in the business.
- Record any changes to the official name of the business not recorded elsewhere as well as any popular or common names by which the business has been known.
- Record any other important information not recorded elsewhere in the administrative history.
- In all the above, include dates, especially dates of birth and death. If you don't have solid dates, estimate years and decades as closely as you can.

For example:

The Woodbury Granite Company started as the Voodry and Town Granite Company, a single quarry on twenty-five acres on Robeson Mountain in Woodbury, Vermont, opened in the early 1880s by George B. Voodry and H. W. Town. In 1888, Alfred and Charles Watson and William Fullerton bought it and incorporated it as the Woodbury Granite Company. In 1895, John S. Holden (1845–1907) and Charles W. Leonard (1844–1941), new owners of the Hardwick and Woodbury Railroad, acquired it. In 1897, Holden's brother Daniel (1850–1939), moved to Hardwick and concentrated on modernizing the quarry operation so The Company, as it was called, could use it for cutting large monuments and mausoleums. The Company added land and buildings, including a boarding house at the quarry site for workers. By 1904, The Company had 135 acres, five buildings, and a network of railroad tracks at the quarry site.

The owners deferred making a decision about whether to build the main office and cutting plant in Hardwick or Woodbury while the people of Hardwick debated whether to build a tax-funded electric power plant. The villagers' decision to build the power plant came on July 26, 1897, and The Company immediately announced it would locate its operation in the village of Hardwick. In late 1897, Holden's son-in-law, twenty-nine-year-old George Hamilton Bickford, (1868–1914) moved his family to Hardwick and replaced Daniel Holden as general manager and treasurer; Holden went into real estate.

With the quarrying operation established, The Company management created a partnership with Charles Herbert More (1857–1939), of Barre, who had vast experience in the granite-cutting business. The partners created a new company, Bickford, More, and Company, to handle the cutting operation. They quickly found that the cost of managing two companies put a strain on their financial backers, so in 1902, they rolled Bickford, More, and Company into the Woodbury Granite Company to create greater efficiency.

Under Bickford's direct management and salesmanship, and indirect leadership of Holden and the financial connections Leonard had access to, The Company quickly became a major player in the building granite industry. It established its reputation when it completed quarrying, cutting, shipping, and putting in place the 400,000 cubic feet of granite for the Pennsylvania State Capitol two months earlier than the two-year contract signed in March 1903 called for. It was the largest granite contract ever offered, and most in the industry regarded it as impossible to meet.

Later in 1903, The Company bought a quarry and built a cutting plant in Bethel, Vermont. A few years later, it bought a cutting plant in Northfield, Vermont. The Company had branch offices in Pittsburgh, New York City, Chicago, and Washington, D.C., but it kept its home office in Hardwick. It became a vertically integrated enterprise owning quarries, cutting sheds, offices, power plants, forests and saw mills for its lumber needs, and pastures for its work animals. Though The Company did not design buildings, Bickford worked with the outstanding architects of the day. After The Company had signed a contract, it took responsibility for a project, from turning architectural drawings into designs for hundreds of individual stones to sending erecting crews on site and putting the stones in place.

In 1912, The Company signed a contract on a new building every three days. A partial list of projects published in 1914, shows it had built four state capitols; five city halls, including Chicago City Hall and Cook County Court House; five post offices; sixteen banks; thirteen commercial buildings; two railroad stations, including Union Station in Washington, D.C.; three high schools; ten memorial sites, including the Navy Memorial in the Vicksburg (MS) National Military Park; two museums, including the Museum of Fine Arts in Minneapolis; Pro-Cathedral in Minneapolis; the Connecticut State Library; and the Harry Payne Whitney Residence in New York City.

From the beginning, The Company accepted unionization, and its labor contracts invariably followed those in Barre, Vermont, which had a much larger granite industry focused largely on monuments and architectural trim pieces. Because of The Company's size in Hardwick—its tax valuation represented 64 percent of the total value of the thirteen companies in Hardwick in 1910—its contract became the default labor contract for all firms in the area. The Company generally enjoyed good relations with the unions and advertized its unionized work as a mark of quality. A 1907 state report on the economic impact of the granite industry in Vermont shows The Company as virtually the only company producing building granite. It added just over $1,000,000 to the state economy that year.

In 1914, Bickford died of appendicitis and peritonitis, leaving the company without inspired leadership; Holden had died in 1907. William Charles Clifford (1870–1937), manager of the Bethel branch, became general manager and shifted the focus of The Company from Hardwick to Bethel.

The advent of World War I marked the beginning of the end of granite buildings with low profiles and big footprints in favor of tall skyscrapers with small footprints for commercial and government buildings. The AT&T building, erected in New York City in 1922, became the last large building The Company built. It revitalized its mausoleum business after World War I, but the Depression ended the market for that.

While we don't have good documentation on the demise of The Company as the complicated vertically integrated entity of the prewar years, surviving records show that by 1935, John B. Hall and Associates had acquired the real estate and equipment that remained of The Company. Hall changed its name, thereby ending the existence of the Woodbury Granite Company

Describing your materials greatly expedites processing and enables professionals to find them on the shelf for researchers.

Describing Museum Objects

Museum objects don't tell their own story the way documents do. Instead, they earn their place in a museum's collection because they (1) represent a type of something, for example, a set of skis from the 1920s; (2) they got caught up in an important event, for example, a twisted business sign found after Hurricane Irma passed over the American Virgin Islands in 2017; or (3) played an important role in the life or work of a famous/important person, for example, George Washington's false teeth.

The museum profession does not have a single comprehensive description standard, so we have used elements from several standards to create the list of pieces of information you should collect about the artifacts you have.[2]

- Name or type of the object
- If part of a larger set, describe the set
- Materials or processes used to create it/them
- Place of manufacture/creation
- Maker/Artist/Designer/Manufacturer/Distributor and dates
- Place of use and dates
- Association with person(s) place, event, or social/ethnic, or other group
- Story behind any markings or inscriptions
- Other comments

Name or type of the object:	Place settings of tableware
If part of a larger set, describe the set:	One of a collection of five
Materials or processes used to create it/them:	Pewter plate, 3-tined pewter fork, and pewter spoon
Place of manufacture/creation Maker/Artist/Designer/Manufacturer/Distributor and dates:	Unknown, probably Connecticut
	Unknown maker dating to the last quarter of the eighteenth century
Users and dates:	Used by the Robert Garfield family before the Civil War
Place of use and dates:	The Garfields moved from Litchfield County, Connecticut to Bridport, Vermont in 1794.

Association with person(s) place, event, or social/ethnic, etc. group:	Typical of early pioneers of the area and era
Story behind any markings or inscriptions:	N/A
Chain of ownership (provenance):	When they could afford better tableware, the Garfields put these in the attic of the farm house. The farm and house passed down through the youngest son's family (Samuel Garfield, to David Garfield, to Mary Anne Garfield Cross) until it was sold in the 1930s. Sandra Cross, oldest daughter of Mary Anne Garfield Cross, donated these to the museum in 1957.
Other comments	None

Step 2: Find a Place That Wants It

After you know what you have, you can start looking for an institutional home for it. Start by deciding on an archive or a museum. Dividing your materials among different institutions diminishes the value of all of them—remember that complete collections are better than incomplete or fragmented collections. Occasionally, you may find specific reasons to break off a part of a collection to go to a repository away from the rest of the collection, but not usually.

When you start looking for an institution, think about where your materials "belong." Generally, professionals agree that materials, with the exception of letters, belong at their place of origin; letters belong where they were received. But, while the place-of-origin rule provides guidance, you should not overinterpret it. For instance, family and financial records or store apparatus from an early country store in a rural part of New England would "belong" equally well in the town's historical society, in the state's historical society, in the state university's special collections, or in a collection of New England business records. They will never belong in a repository in Iowa—unless the owners moved from New England and settled in Iowa and opened a store there. Sometimes, your materials belong in a place that no longer has any residents with a direct connection to the materials.

So, make a list of the places that your materials might appeal to. Take your time to consider all possibilities. Research your choices by looking over the mission statement and collections policy; most institutions now post them online. Look at the collections the institution holds. Look at the description of the major collection(s) and ask why they belong there. Think about how your materials fit into a particular institution's collection.

Museums use a variety of criteria when deciding to accept donations: What does the donor have to offer? What are they made of and what condition are they in? Do they fit into our collection? How will we use this material to further our mission? Were the materials made locally, owned and/or used by someone local. Are these materials unique to our area? What story do the materials tell and how is that story related to our mission? Can we tell the story of the owners using these materials? How will the materials enhance or add to our existing collections? Do they have historical significance? If so, to whom? About what? Are the materials unusual?

Are the artifacts whole or complete? Does it matter? Will the materials require special care or need conservation attention? Can we take care of these materials? How much space do the materials take up? Do we have the space to store or exhibit them? Could we use these materials in an exhibit? Do the materials have any restrictions attached to their use? Does the donor want something we can't give or guarantee in return for the gift? Might another institution be a better place for this material? If these materials are being offered for sale, do we have the funding to purchase these materials or could we raise the funds within a reasonable time? Is the material worth the effort? It can get complicated.

If you decide to visit a repository with donating in mind, look for the following impressions and information: First, will it survive? Some historical societies and local museums may not have much future because they lack funding; leadership; city, county, and/or state support; professional guidance; or some other circumstance. You want to make sure the repository you choose will last well into the future and take good care of your donation. Look for indications that the historical society, museum, archive, or institution is viable. Ask someone knowledgeable about the organization such questions as: Does the organization have a governing body? Are they a nonprofit? Do they have future plans? Do they have regular business meetings? Are they engaged with the community? Then look at the building and facility itself. Do displays and exhibits look clean and well cared for? Does the institution keep regular hours? Do the staff and volunteers appear engaged in their activities? Does the building look well cared for? Do they have secure and clean storage areas in the museum?

While we stated a few pages ago that you should not divide up collections, some circumstances make that acceptable. If, for instance, you have

The collections storage area in the Center for Popular Music, Middle Tennessee State University, Murfreesboro.
From the Collections of the Center for Popular Music, Middle Tennessee State University, Murfreesboro.

duplicate materials, you might place a set of duplicates in a repository that has a specific connection to those materials. If you have materials in your collection that do not relate closely to the rest of the collection or actually belong in another place or collection, you could donate them to a more appropriate repository. You might find a sub-collection from a specific person for which the person's alma mater or a professional organization might be a more appropriate repository. You might find a cache of materials that has no relation to any of the people in your family, but which could enhance the collections at another repository. For instance, a collection of postcards that does not include any personal correspondence to or from members of your family might better go to a repository that collects postcards similar to the materials that you have.

The records of a very early community church appeared in the papers of one of the leaders of the frontier community who had also held many positions of leadership in the church. When his papers went to the state university's Special Collections Department, the processors separated the church records into their own collection.

After settling on a few institutions, write a letter or an email giving a brief description of your collection so the institution has a general idea about what you are offering. Include a few photos to clarify your description, then ask if the collection appeals to them. Send the letter to the director, a curator, or an archivist at the repository. A letter or email allows the recipient time to consider a response and to check with others, if the repository requires that. A written request also assures that everyone has the same details about the request; we know how word-of-mouth descriptions given in a telephone conversation can become distorted.

After you have sent your letter, be patient. Your contact may have to get authorization from a superior, but if you don't hear anything in a month or so, follow up. If the repository does not have any interest, ask for suggestions of other, more suitable repositories; don't take the rejection personally.

If the repository expresses interest, your contact person will explain the repository's procedure for accepting materials. Most institutions have a set of policies and procedures for acquiring materials, and your contact will walk you through them.

Step 3: Take Care of Business

APPRAISALS

No matter whether you plan to donate or sell materials, consider getting an appraisal. A professional appraiser can assign a monetary value to the materials in your collections and help you make informed decisions based on their value. The IRS Publication 561 makes clear that the archive or museum receiving the materials cannot make the appraisal.[3]

In most cases, you need a Personal Property Appraiser specializing in manuscripts, household contents, art, etc. Look for one who has certification from one of the professional appraisers' organizations listed in "Resources" later in this chapter. Each organization has an online directory you can use to find an appraiser who can meet your needs. When you have located some prospects, get to know them. Ask as many questions as you want so you get a sense of his or her fit with your situation. Don't be shy; you will pay for his or her expertise and experience, and you want to make sure it suits your needs.

At this point in the process, you need a fairly informal appraisal. Your appraiser could help you to decide whether to donate or sell your materials, so talk with the appraiser before you talk to your tax professional. Unless you plan to sell your materials, you don't need a formal appraisal for tax purposes. You just need the appraiser's professional advice, which will take a few hours of your appraiser's time. If you plan to donate your materials to an institution, ask the appraiser for a professional opinion as to whether the materials that you want to donate will benefit from a formal appraisal. That is, will the materials have a monetary value greater than the cost of a formal appraisal? Ask the appraiser for a listing of the pieces she or he identifies as worthy of a formal appraisal. Appraisers are not dealers. For this process you will need an appraiser—a professional, independent, impartial valuator of your materials—not a dealer.

APPRAISALS FOR DONATION OR SALE

Regardless whether you plan to donate or sell your materials, you want to know the Fair Market Value. The IRS defines Fair Market Value as "the price at which property would change hands between a willing buyer and a willing seller, neither being under any compulsion to buy or sell and both having reasonable knowledge of the relevant facts."[4] The worth of most items in your attic will depend on the price of similar items of the same age and condition at a recent auction or in an open sale.

If you plan to sell your materials, you should have a formal appraisal so that you can set your price based on current information about fair market value and can determine what reasonable counteroffer a museum or archives might make. Bear in mind that an appraiser cannot give you a current fair market value without time and research—values can change rapidly.

As we said earlier, if an institution agrees to buy your materials, it may need time to raise the money. Consider getting a written agreement that gives a specified period for the institution to raise funds. After that time, the agreement will release you from any obligation to sell, and it will release the institution from its obligation to buy.

If you donate your family materials, you do not need a formal appraisal, but an appraiser can guide you through the donation process and make sure that your donation meets the IRS requirements for noncash charitable donations.

TAXES

As your appraiser will confirm, historically significant materials can have monetary value, and with monetary value come tax ramifications. Whether you want to donate materials, sell them, or a combination of both, you should learn about the tax benefits and liabilities of your actions. A tax adviser can help you to evaluate whether a noncash charitable deduction from your taxes would be more valuable to you than income received from the sale of materials to a repository.

If you decide to use a tax adviser, make sure that he or she understands the Internal Revenue Service (IRS) rulings on non-cash charitable deductions—not all tax advisers deal with non-cash charitable deductions. You should also become familiar with the following IRS publications: Publication 526, *Charitable Contributions*, Publication 561, *Determining the Value of Donated Property*, and Publication 8283, *Non-cash Charitable Deductions*.[5]

These documents tell you what records you need to keep, what tax deductions you may take, and other important details, such as timing considerations in relation to tax deductions and appraisals. Reading them will give you some background understanding to take into your meeting with a tax adviser. Tax laws change, so make sure you read the newest versions of the publications.

The IRS considers a gift completed when you receive a deed of gift. Like a bill of sale, a deed of gift legally transfers the title or ownership and all rights that go with ownership from the donor to the receiving institution. The IRS considers the date on the deed of gift the date of the gift.

Step 4: Send It Off

After the repository confirms that it would like to accept your material, you'll need to pack and ship it. Your contact person at the institution will have had experience and can give you guidance about what the repository wants you to do. Ask about insurance. Ask what costs the repository will cover. Museums and archives normally will not cover shipping costs, but some will—there's no harm in asking. If you have objects that require special packing, you should discuss this with your contact. The institution may have resources to help with packing. If you have donated your materials to a nearby institution, ask if their representative will pack or pick up your materials. In each container, include a rough inventory of the contents. Keep a copy for yourself, and send a full set to your contact.

The repository will send you a deed of gift or a bill of sale. Because those documents formally acknowledge that the repository has received your collection and taken ownership of it, ask your appraiser or tax adviser how to proceed with responding to any tax implications.

SUPPORT FOR CATALOGING AND CARE

Consider making a donation to the repository to support the cataloging and care of your gift. Most museums and archives, no matter how well funded, have a backlog of materials that need processing, and they usually do not have enough staff to do the work. Further, the cost of supplies for safely housing collections can add up quickly. The perfect donor recognizes that by donating your *stuff*, you have done the receiving repository a favor by enhancing its collections, and that the repository has done you a favor by providing your family a form of immortality. Even if you can give only a token amount, your gift will create goodwill and serve as an acknowledgment that you understand that your donation both enhances the collections and adds to the repository's responsibilities.

If you can afford to, consider setting up a fund for your collection, especially if you have donated a large collection. Also, if you donate something like a library, let the receiving repository know that they have your approval to sell items they cannot use. Ask the repository to use any funds received in such a sale for the care for the collection.

Step 5: Notify All Interested Parties

When everything has gone out the door, notify your family and all other interested parties about what you have done. In doing so, let everyone know what materials you sent where, and how they may access them.

The letter should list all receiving institutions, including their addresses along with any information that seems pertinent. If an archive has restricted access, explain how a family member can gain access, for example, forms needed for permission to use the archive. If you know of any other places that have materials related to your family—materials that did not come from you—include a list of those institutions. Finally, list everyone a copy of your letter and encourage who received them to send the letter onto others they think should know this information.

Your letter assures that all interested parties know what has been done, and it prevents rumors and misunderstandings within the family.

Vusi and his sister Ophelia donated their grandfather's papers, photographs, and music to a local university archive after years of keeping them in their grandmother's garage. Their grandfather had been a prominent local jazz and blues musician and his wife had been diligent about keeping everything. It was a large and rich collection and it took the university archivist two years to process it and make it available to the public. Ophelia and other family members asked to see some of the documents and photographs and were pleased at the result, especially since the collection was getting regular use by students, professors, and researchers. Vusi, however, lived in South Africa, and he voiced his displeasure at not being able to access his grandfather's materials. Ophelia told him he could view the collection next time he visited the States. Vusi lamented that he is not allowed to view the materials even if he visited the United States because he was a citizen of South Africa. When Ophelia asked the archivist about this rule, she learned that Vusi was wrong. The grandfather's papers were open to anyone, and the university would especially welcome Vusi. Ophelia relayed this fact to Vusi, who was delighted to hear it. It seemed one of his South African friends told him he would not be able to access the archives, thus the misunderstanding. Ophelia had been in charge of most of the paperwork and legal dealings associated with the donation of the materials and had not thought to send out a letter to all family members outlining the open access policy of the collection.

RESOURCES

The Society of American Archivists. "Donating Your Personal or Family Records to a Repository." Accessed December 28, 2017. https://www2 .archivists.org/publications/brochures/donating-familyrecs.

Appraisal Organizations

American Society of Appraisers. http://www.appraisers.org.
Appraisers Association. https://www.appraisersassociation.org.
The International Society of Appraisers. http://www.isa-appraisers .org.
The Appraisal Foundation. *2018–2019 Uniform Standards of Professional Appraisal Practice (USPAP).* http://www.uspap.org.

NOTES

1. Society of American Archivists, *Describing Archives: A Content Standard (DACS)* (Chicago: Author, 2013), 34–44), accessed December 28. 2017, http://www.files. archivists.org/pubs/DACS2E-2013_v0315.pdf.

2. Daniel B. Reibel, *Registration Methods for the Small Museum,* fourth edition (American Association for State and Local History Book series) (Lanham, MD: AltaMira, 2008); International Council on Museums, and International Committee for Documentation, *CIDOC-CRM* v.5.0.4 (2011) http://www.cidoc-crm.org; Baca Murtha, et al., eds., *Cataloging Cultural Objects: A Guide to Describing Cultural Work*

and Images (Chicago: American Library Association/Visual Resources Association, 2006).

    3. Internal Revenue Service, Publication 561, *Determining the Value of Donated Property*. https://www.irs.gov/pub/irs-pdf/p516.pdf.

    4. Ibid.

    5. Internal Revenue Service, Publication 526, *Charitable Contributions*, https://www.irs.gov/pub/irs-pdf/p526.pdf; Publication 828, *Non-cash Charitable Deductions*, https://www.irs.gov/pub/irs-pdf/p8283.pdf.

Index

About the Authors

Elizabeth H. Dow discovered during her last class toward a PhD at the University of Pittsburgh's School of Library and Information Science that she could blend her love of history and love of organizing information by becoming an archivist. Subsequently, she worked as an archivist at the Henry Sheldon Museum in Middlebury, Vermont, the Vermont State Archives, and the Special Collections Division of the University of Vermont's Bailey/Howe Library. In 2001, she left Vermont to create the archives track in Louisiana State University's School of Library and Information Science. She retired as the J. Franklin Bayhi Professor of Library and Information Science in 2014, and moved back home to Hardwick, Vermont. She is the author of *Creating EAD-Compatible Finding Guides on Paper* (Scarecrow, 2005), *Electronic Records in the Manuscript Repository* (Scarecrow, 2009), and *Archivists, Collectors, Dealers, and Replevin: Case Studies on Private Ownership of Public Documents* (Scarecrow, 2012).

Lucinda P. Cockrell has worked professionally for more than thirty years in the museum, archives, and public history field. She has degrees in historic preservation and museum education, and is a certified archivist. Her career has been graced by positions held at the James K. Polk Ancestral Home (Columbia, Tennessee), the Yorktown (Virginia) Victory Center, and the Center for Popular Music at Middle Tennessee State University. She now lives in the mountains of Vermont with her husband, Dale, and her dog, Enkidu, and volunteers in local museums and libraries, serves on boards, collects ephemera, and helps friends weed their attics.